# Automobile Maintenance, including: Car Talk, Jump Start (vehicle), Timing Belt, Tire Rotation, Oil Sludge, Auto Detailing, User Guide, Car Wash, Grease Gun (tool), Back-fire, Cold Inflation Pressure, Haynes Manual, Wheel Alignment, Auto Mechanic, Rain-x

Hephaestus Books

# Contents

## Articles

# Car Talk

## Car Talk

| Genre | Automotive repair/advice, Humor |
|---|---|
| **Running time** | ca. 50 min |
| **Country** | United States |
| **Languages** | English |
| **Home station** | WBUR |
| **Syndicates** | National Public Radio |
| **Hosts** | Tom Magliozzi<br>Ray Magliozzi |
| **Producers** | Doug "The Subway Fugitive, Not A Slave To Fashion, Bongo Boy" Berman |
| **Recording studio** | Cambridge, Massachusetts |
| **Air dates** | 1977 to *present* |
| **Audio format** | Stereophonic |
| **Opening theme** | "Dawggy Mountain Breakdown", David Grisman, composer |
| **Other themes** | B.J. Leiderman (composer) |
| **Website** | http://www.cartalk.com |

***Car Talk*** is a radio talk show broadcast weekly on National Public Radio stations throughout the United States and elsewhere. Its subjects are automobiles and repair, and it often takes humorous turns. The hosts of Car Talk are brothers Tom and Ray Magliozzi, also known as *Click and Clack, the Tappet Brothers*.

# Show

*Car Talk* is structured as a call-in radio show: listeners call with questions related to motor vehicle maintenance and repair. Most of the advice sought is diagnostic, with callers describing symptoms and demonstrating sounds of an ailing vehicle while the Magliozzis make an attempt at identifying the malfunction. While the hosts pepper their call-in sessions with jokes directed at both the caller and at themselves, the depth and breadth of their knowledge of automobiles is extensive, and they are usually able to arrive at a diagnosis and give helpful advice. Also, if a caller has an unusual name, they will inquire about the spelling, pronunciation, and/or origin of their name. They may also comment about the caller's hometown. The Magliozzis previously took a break at approximately the half-hour mark of the show. More recently, two breaks divide the show into approximately 20-minute segments referred to as the "three halves" of the show. Between segments a piece of music, usually related to cars in some way, will play. One example was "Fast Cars" by The Buzzcocks.

*Car Talk* was first broadcast on WBUR in Boston in 1977. It was picked up nationally by NPR ten years later. NPR reports that it is heard on more than 370 stations by an audience of more than two million weekly listeners. The show is also carried on Sirius XM Satellite Radio via both the NPR Now and NPR Talk channels. These two NPR stations rebroadcast the show throughout the weekend.

The show was the inspiration for the short-lived "George Wendt Show", which aired on CBS in the 1995-96 season.

In May 2007, the program, which had only previously been available digitally as a paid subscription from Audible.com, became a free podcast distributed by NPR, after a two-month test period where only a "call of the week" was available via podcast.

The *Car Talk* theme song is "Dawggy Mountain Breakdown" by bluegrass artist David Grisman.

# Call-in procedure

Throughout the program, listeners are encouraged to dial the toll-free telephone number, 1-888-CAR-TALK (1-888-227-8255), which connects to a 24-hour answering service. Although the approximately 2,000 queries received each week are screened by the *Car Talk* staff, the questions are unknown to the Magliozzis in advance as "that would entail researching the right answer, which is what? ...Work." Producers select and contact the callers several days ahead of the show's Wednesday taping to arrange the segment. The caller speaks briefly to a producer before being connected "live" with the hosts, and is given little coaching other than being told to be prepared to talk, not to use any written preparation and to "have fun". The show deliberately tapes more callers than they have time to air each week in order to be able to choose the best ones for broadcast. Those segments that do make it to air are generally edited for time.

## Features

The show opens with a short comedy segment, typically jokes sent in by listeners, followed by eight call-in sessions. The hosts run a contest called the "Puzzler", in which a riddle, sometimes car related, is presented. The answer to the previous week's "Puzzler" is given at the beginning of the "second half" of the show, and a new puzzler is given at the start of the "third half". The hosts give instructions to listeners to write answers addressed to "Puzzler Tower" on some non-existent or expensive object, such as a 26-dollar bill or an advanced SLR digital camera. This gag initially started as suggesting that the answers be written "on the back of a twenty dollar bill."

A recurring feature is "Stump the Chumps", in which they revisit a caller from a previous show to determine the effect, if any, of their advice. A similar feature began in May 2001, "Where Are They Now, Tommy?"

Celebrities have been callers as well. Examples include Geena Davis, Morley Safer, Ashley Judd, Gordon Elliott, former Major League pitcher Bill Lee and astronaut John Grunsfeld calling from the Space Shuttle. There have been numerous appearances from NPR personalities, including Bob Edwards, Susan Stamberg, Scott Simon, Ray Suarez, Will Shortz, Sylvia Poggioli, and commentator and author Daniel Pinkwater. On one occasion, the show featured Martha Stewart as an in-studio guest, whom the Magliozzis twice during the segment referred to as "Margaret".

In addition to at least one on-orbit call, the Brothers once received a call asking advice on winterizing a couple of "kit cars". After much beating around the bush and increasing evasiveness by the caller, they asked him just how much these kit cars were worth. The answer: about $800 million. It was a joke call from the Jet Propulsion Laboratory concerning the preparation of the Mars Rovers (*Spirit* and *Opportunity*) for the oncoming Martian winter. Click and Clack have also been featured in editorial cartoons, including one where a befuddled NASA engineer calls them to ask how to fix the Space Shuttle.

## Humor

Leading into each break in the show, one of the hosts leads up to the network identification with a humorous take on a disgusted reaction of some usually famous person to hearing that identification. The full line goes along the pattern of, for example, "And even though Roger Clemens stabs his radio with a syringe whenever he hears *us* say it, this is NPR: National Public Radio."

Other humor exists throughout. The end credits feature a rotating list of puns and wordplay. At some point in almost every show, usually when giving the address for the Puzzler answers, Ray will mention Cambridge, Massachusetts (where the show originates) at which point Tom reverently interjects "our fair city."

They are known for their self-deprecating humor, often joking about their poor advice. They also comment at the end of each show: "Well, it's happened again - you've squandered another perfectly good hour listening to *Car Talk*."

The ending credits of the show start with the colorfully nicknamed actual staffers (notably producer "Doug the subway fugitive, not a slave to fashion, bongo boy Berman" and "John 'Bugsy' Lawlor, just back from the..." every week a different eating event with rhyming foodstuff names), but soon turn into a lengthy list of pun-filled fictional staffers and sponsors such as statistician Marge Innovera ("margin of error"), meteorologist Claudio Vernight ("cloudy overnight"), optometric firm C.F. Eye Care ("see if I care"), Russian chauffeur Pickup Andropov ("pick up and drop off"), and law firm Dewey, Cheetham and Howe ("Do we cheat 'em and how").

At the end of the show, Ray warns the audience, "Don't drive like my brother," to which Tom replies, "And don't drive like *my* brother." Earlier, this was phrased "Don't drive like a knucklehead." There have been variations—such as, "Don't drive like my brother..." "And don't drive like his brother," and "Don't drive like my sister..." "And don't drive like *my* sister". The tagline was heard in a cameo for the Pixar film *Cars*, in which Tom and Ray voiced anthropomorphized vehicles (Rusty and Dusty Rust-Eze, a 1963 Dodge Dart V1.0 and a 1963 Dodge A100 van respectively) with personalities similar to their own on-air personae. Tom notoriously once owned a green Dodge Dart, known as the "Dartre".

## Hosts

Main articles: Tom Magliozzi and Ray Magliozzi

The Magliozzis are long-time car mechanics. Ray Magliozzi has a bachelor of science degree in humanities and science from MIT, while Tom has a bachelor of science degree in economics from MIT and an MBA and DBA from the Boston University Graduate School of Management.

The duo, usually led by Ray, are known for rants on the evils of the internal combustion engine, people who talk on cell phones while driving, Peugeots, women named Donna who always seem to drive Camaros, the clever use of the English language, and practically anything

The name of the DC&H corporate offices is visible on the third floor window above the corner of Brattle and JFK Streets, in Harvard Square, Cambridge, Massachusetts.

else, including themselves. They have a relaxed and humorous approach to cars, car repair, cup holders, pets, lawyers, car repair mechanics, SUVs, and almost everything else. They often cast a critical, jaundiced insider's eye toward the auto industry. Tom and Ray are committed to the values of defensive driving and environmentalism.

The Magliozzis operate the Good News Garage in Cambridge, Massachusetts, a few blocks northwest of the MIT campus. The show's offices are located nearby at the corner of JFK Street and Brattle Street in Harvard Square, marked as "Dewey, Cheetham & Howe", the imaginary law firm to which they refer on-air. DC&H doubles as the business name of Tappet Brothers Associates, the corporation established to manage the business end of *Car Talk*. Initially a joke, the company was incorporated after the show expanded from a single station to national syndication.

The two were commencement speakers at MIT in 1999.

## *Click and Clack's As the Wrench Turns*

Main article: Click and Clack's As the Wrench Turns

On July 11, 2007, PBS announced that it had greenlit an animated adaptation of *Car Talk*, to air on prime-time in 2008. The show is entitled *Click and Clack's As the Wrench Turns*, and is based on the adventures of the fictional "Click and Clack" brothers' garage at "Car Talk Plaza". The first episode aired on July 9, 2008.

## External links

- *Car Talk* official website [1]
- *Car Talk* Podcasting Page [2]
- *Car Talk* History [3]
- *Click and Clack's As the Wrench Turns* official website [4]
- Exhaustive list of *Car Talk* credits [5]
- Transcript of the Magliozzis' commencement address at MIT, 1999 [6]

# Jump start (vehicle)

## Jump start (vehicle)

A **jump start**, also called a **boost**, is a method of starting an automobile or other vehicle powered by an internal combustion engine when the vehicle's battery has been discharged. A second battery (often in another vehicle) is temporarily connected to provide starting power to the disabled vehicle. Once the disabled vehicle's engine is running, its alternator or generator should recharge the dead battery, so the second battery can now be disconnected.

Most passenger vehicles use a 12-volt car battery that provides power to a starting electric motor for the engine. When the engine is running, electrical power from its alternator restores the charge to the battery in preparation for the next start. When a battery is discharged, as for example by headlights left on while the engine is off, the car's engine will not "turn over" when the ignition key is turned and the vehicle will not start.

### Jumper cables

Many motorists carry jumper cables (UK usage: jump leads) which consist of a pair of heavy gauge, insulated wires with alligator clips at each end. Jumper cables are available in various lengths. The size of copper conductors varies from about #10 AWG for light duty sets, to #1 AWG. The alligator clips generally have color-coded, vinyl-coated (PVC) insulation to prevent electrical short circuits. Most clips fit both top- and side-mounted battery terminals. Top-quality clips are made of solid copper; lesser-quality are made of

Jumper cable connected to positive post

material such as copper-plated steel. Jumper cables are marked by black (-) and red (+) handles, representing the two polarities of the automobile's direct current system. Interchanging the polarities will cause a short circuit and a hazard to people and damage to one or both automobiles, possibly including blown electrical fuses and circuit boards. Car manuals recommend connecting the negative (black) cable last and disconnecting it first, since otherwise the battery may be shorted by the tool used to loosen the cable clamps. Connecting the positive (red) cable while the negative cable is connected can also cause a spark, resulting in battery explosion.

# Limitations

Operation of a lead-acid battery may, in case of overcharge, produce flammable hydrogen gas by electrolysis of water inside the battery. Jump start procedures are usually found in the vehicle owner's manual. The recommended sequence of connections is intended to reduce the chance of accidentally shorting the good battery or igniting hydrogen gas. Owner's manuals will show the preferred locations for connection of jumper cables; for example, some vehicles have the battery mounted under a seat, or may have a jumper terminal in the engine compartment.

Motorists can be severely injured by a battery explosion. In the United States in 1994, a research note by the National Highway Traffic Safety Association estimated that about 442 persons were injured by exploding batteries while attempting a jump-start.

Current from the boosting vehicle will charge the dead battery. After several minutes enough energy is transferred to allow cranking of the engine. If the connections are good and the cables are large, the boosting vehicle battery may also supply part of the cranking current. In an extreme case, it is possible to crank and start a vehicle with no battery in it if the cables are heavy-duty. Cranking current drawn through light-gauge cables in this way will damage them by overheating; electrical resistance of a smaller wire is higher than that of a larger wire, and resistance dissipates electrical energy into heat.

If the discharged battery case is cracked, or the battery has a low electrolyte level, or is frozen, a jump start will not restore normal operation. A jump start is only effective for a discharged battery and cannot resolve other faults including a lack of fuel, a failed battery, or other mechanical problems. Even after a successful jump start a vehicle may not be able to resume normal operation if the reason for the dead battery is a failed charging system. Loss of voltage from the vehicle battery may have wide-ranging effects—from a trivial loss of radio receiver preset stations to a significant loss of security codes or engine control parameters.

# Motorcycles

Many very old motorcycles (and cars) have 6-volt systems and cannot be jump started safely with a modern car, but newer designs with 12-volt systems may be jump started with a 12-volt car or truck. Car batteries can generally jump start a motorcycle easily without any help from the car's alternator. An alternative is to push start the motorcycle.

# Alternatives to jumper cables

## Cigarette lighter outlet

An alternative to jumper cables is a cable used to interconnect the 12 volt power outlets (cigarette lighter outlets) of two vehicles. While this eliminates concerns with incorrect connections and generation of arcs near battery terminals, the amount of current available through such a connection is small. This method works by slowly recharging the battery, not by providing the current needed for cranking. Engine cranking should not be attempted as the starter motor current will exceed the fuse rating in a cigarette lighter outlet. Many vehicles turn off the cigarette lighter outlets when the key is turned off, making the technique unusable unless the ignition key is turned to the accessory or on position to connect the cigarette lighter outlet to the battery.

## Battery booster and jump starter

A hand-portable battery, equipped with attached cables and charger, can be used similarly to another vehicle's battery.

Portable boosters may automatically sense the battery's polarity prior to sending power to the vehicle, eliminating the damage that can result from reversing the connection.

## Battery charger

Motorists and service garages often have portable battery chargers operated from AC power. Very small "trickle" chargers are intended only to maintain a charge on a parked or stored vehicle, but larger chargers can put enough charge into a battery to allow a start within a few minutes. Battery chargers may be strictly manual, or may include controls for time and charging voltage. Some chargers are equipped with "boost" settings that supply a large current to assist in cranking the engine. Battery chargers that apply high voltage (for example, more than 16 volts on a 12 volt nominal system) will result in high emission of hydrogen gas from the battery and may damage it. A battery may be recharged without removal from the vehicle, although in a typical roadside situation no convenient source of AC power may be nearby.

## Push starting

Main article: Push start

A vehicle with a manual transmission may be push started. This requires caution while pushing the vehicle and may require the assistance of several persons. If the vehicle battery cannot provide power to the ignition system, push starting will be ineffective. Most vehicles with automatic transmissions cannot be started this way because the hydraulic torque converter in the transmission will not allow the engine to be driven by the wheels (some very old automatic transmissions, e.g., General Motors' two-speed Powerglide transmission, do leave a solid connection between the engine and wheels, and cars equipped with such transmissions can be push started).

# Voltage problem

Formerly, especially in cold climates, some jump starts were done with two series-connected batteries to provide 24 volts to a 12 volt starting motor. However, such overvoltage can cause severe and expensive damage to the electronic systems on modern automobiles and should never be used.

Heavy vehicles such as large trucks, excavation equipment, or vehicles with diesel engines may use 24-volt electrical systems. These cannot be boosted from a 12-volt motor vehicle and must not be used to boost a 12-volt motor vehicle.

Vintage cars may have 6-volt electrical systems, or may connect the positive terminal of the battery to the chassis. The methods intended for boosting 12-volt, negative-ground vehicles cannot be used in such cases.

Passenger vehicles with 42-volt electrical systems may not be possible to "boost" from other vehicles; professional assistance would be required to prevent severe damage to the vehicle and possible personal injury (see tow truck). Hybrid vehicles may have a very small 12 volt battery system unsuitable for sourcing the large amount of current required to boost a conventional vehicle. However, as the 12-volt system of a hybrid vehicle is only required to start up the control system of the vehicle, a very small portable battery may successfully boost a hybrid that has accidentally discharged its 12-volt system; the main propulsion battery is unlikely to also have been discharged.

# Military vehicles

Generally referred to as "slave starting" in military parlance, the jump starting procedure has been simplified for military vehicles. Tactical vehicles used by NATO militaries possess 24-volt electrical systems and, in accordance with STANAG 4074, have standard slave receptacles for easy connection. A slave cable is plugged in to the receptacle on each vehicle, and the dead vehicle is started with the live vehicle's engine running.

Slave receptacle on an M1009 CUCV

## See also

- Crocodile clip used in the cables.

## External links

- Breakdown Advice : using jump leads safely - The AA (United Kingdom) [1]
- do-it-yourself jump start [4]
- Official Car Talk Guide to Jump Starting Your Car [5] - by Car Talk's Tom and Ray Magliozzi, "Click and Clack, the Tappet Brothers"
- Quick & Easy Directions to Jump Start [6] by Car Care Council

# Timing belt

## Timing belt

A **timing belt**, or **cam belt** (informal usage), is a part of an internal combustion engine that controls the timing of the engine's valves. Some engines, like the flat-4 Volkswagen air cooled engine, and the straight-6 Toyota F engine use timing gears. Timing belts replace the older style timing chains that were in common usage until the 1970's and 1980's (although in the last decade there has been some reemergence of chain use). The term "timing belt" is sometimes used for the more general case of any flat belt with integral teeth, although such usage is a misnomer since there is no timing or synchronization involved.

Timing belt

### Engine applications

In the internal combustion engine application, the timing belt / chain connects the crankshaft to the camshaft(s), which in turn controls the opening and closing of the engine's valves. A four-stroke engine requires that the valves open and close once every other revolution of the crankshaft. The timing belt / chain does this. It has teeth to turn the camshaft(s) synchronised with the crankshaft, and is specifically designed for a particular engine. In some engine designs, the timing belt may also be used to drive other engine components such as the water pump and oil pump.

Gear or chain systems are also used to connect the crankshaft to the camshaft at the correct timing. However gears and shafts constrain the relative location of the crankshaft and camshafts. Even where the                   crankshaft                   and                   camshaft(s)                   are very close together, as in pushrod engines, most engine designers use a short chain drive rather than a direct gear drive. This is because gear drives suffer from frequent torque reversal as the cam profiles "kick back" against the drive from the crank, leading to excessive noise and wear. Fibre gears, with more resilience, are preferred to steel gears where direct drive has to be used. A belt or chain allows much more flexibility in the relative locations of the crankshaft and camshafts.

Timing covers, lower pulley, accessory belts removed, exposing timing belt

While chains and gears may be more durable, rubber composite belts are quieter in their operation (in most modern engines the noise difference is negligible), are less expensive and are mechanically more efficient, by dint of being considerably lighter, when compared with a gear or chain system. Also, timing belts do not require lubrication, which is essential with a timing chain or gears. A timing belt is a specific application of a synchronous belt used to transmit rotational power synchronously.

Timing belts are typically covered by metal or polymer timing belt covers which require removal to carry out inspection or replacement. Engine manufacturers recommend replacement at specific intervals. The manufacturer may also recommend the replacement of other parts, such as the water pump, when the timing belt is replaced because the additional cost to replace the water pump is negligible compared to the cost of accessing the timing belt. In an interference engine, or one whose valves extend into the path of the piston, failure of the timing belt (or timing chain) invariably results in costly and, in some cases, irreparable engine damage, as some valves will be held open when they should not be and thus will be struck by the pistons.

Indicators that the timing chain may need to be replaced include a rattling noise from the front of the engine.

# Timing

When an automotive timing belt is replaced, care must be taken to ensure that the valve and piston movements are correctly synchronized. Failure to synchronize correctly can lead to problems with valve timing, and this in turn, in extremes, can cause collision between valves and pistons in interference engines. This is not a problem unique to timing belts since the same issue exists with all other cam/crank timing methods such as gears or chains.

# Failure

Timing belts must be replaced at the manufacturer's recommended distance and/or time periods. Failure to replace the belt can result in complete breakdown or catastrophic engine failure. The owner's manual maintenance schedule is the source of timing belt replacement intervals, typically every 60,000 to 90,000 miles. It is common to replace the timing belt tensioner at the same time as the belt is replaced.

# Construction & Design

A timing belt is typically rubber with high-tensile fibres (e.g. fiberglass or Twaron / Kevlar) running the length of the belt as tension members.

Older belts have trapezoid shaped teeth leading to high rates of tooth wear. Newer manufacturing techniques allow for curved teeth that are quieter and last longer.

Aftermarket timing belts may be used to alter engine performance. OEM timing belts "will stretch at high rpm, retarding the cam and therefore the ignition. Stronger, aftermarket belts, will not stretch and the timing is preserved. In terms of engine design, "shortening the width of the timing belt reduce[s] weight and friction".

## Usage History

The first known timing belt was used in 1945. The German Glas 1004 was the first mass produced vehicle to use a timing belt in 1962. The first American vehicle to use a timing belt was the 1966 Pontiac Tempest. In 1966, Vauxhall started production of the Slant Four overhead cam four-cylinder design which used a timing belt, a configuration that is now used in the vast majority of cars built today.

# See also

- Gilmer belt
- Interference Engines

# External links

- Timing belt animated diagram [1]
- Charles Ofria (1996). "Timing belt" [2]. *The Family Car web magazine*. SmartTrac Computer Systems, Inc.. Retrieved 2006-06-09.
- Wright brothers' 1903 engine timing system operation [3]
- Troubleshooting timing belt wear [4]
- It's All in the Timing [5] Car Care Council Article

# Tire rotation

## Tire rotation

**Tire rotation** or **rotating tires** is the practice of moving automobile wheels and tires from one position on the car, to another, to ensure even tire wear. Tire wear is uneven for any number of reasons. Even tire wear is desirable to maintain consistent performance in the vehicle and to extend the overall life of a set of tires.

By design, the weight on the front and rear axles differs which causes uneven wear. With the majority of cars being front-engine cars, the front axle typically bears more of the weight. For rear wheel drive vehicles, the weight distribution between front and back approaches 50:50. Front wheel drive vehicles also have the differential in front, adding to the weight, with a typical weight distribution of no better than 60:40. This means, all else being equal, the front tires wear out at almost twice the rate of the rear wheels, especially when factoring the additional stress that braking puts on the front tires. Thus, tire rotation needs to occur more frequently for front-wheel drive vehicles.

Turning the vehicle will cause uneven tire wear. The outside, front tire is worn disproportionately. Cloverleaf interchanges, and parking ramps turn right in left hand drive (otherwise known as right hand traffic) countries, causing the left front tire to be worn faster than the right front. Furthermore, right turns are tighter than left turns, also causing more tire wear. Conversely the sidewalls on the right tire tends to be bumped and rubbed against the curb while parking the vehicle, causing asymmetric sidewall wear. The symmetric opposite occurs in countries that drive on the left.

In addition, mechanical problems in the vehicle may cause uneven tire wear. The wheels need to be aligned with each other and the vehicle. The wheel that is out of alignment will tend to be dragged along by the other wheels, causing uneven wear in that tire. If the alignment is such that the vehicle tends to turn, the driver will correct by steering against the tendency. In effect the vehicle is constantly turning, causing uneven tire wear. Also, if a tire is under or over-inflated, it will wear differently than the other tires on the vehicle. Rotating will not help in this case and the inflation needs to be corrected.

Car manufacturers will recommend tire rotation frequency and pattern. Depending on the specifics of the vehicle, tire rotation may be recommended every 12,000 km (8,000 mi). The rotation pattern is typically moving the back wheels to the front, and the front to the back, but crossing them when moving to the back. If the tires are unidirectional, the rotation can only be rotated front to back on the same side of the vehicle to preserve the rotational direction of the tires. Most unidirectional tires can be moved from side to side if they are remounted; tires with asymmetric rims are a rare exception. More complex rotation patterns are required if the vehicle has a full-size spare tire that is part of the rotation, or if there are snow tires.

To clarify; the pattern for **asymmetrical** tires to be rotated, or positioned, is for the tires on the driving axle of two-wheel drive vehicles to remain on the same side of the vehicle as they are moved to the non-driving axle, and for the tires on the non-driving axle to cross over to the opposite side of the vehicle as they are placed onto the driving axle. For all-wheel drive (AWD) vehicles and four-wheel drive (4WD) vehicles, it is recommended that the tires from each axle cross over as the fronts move to the rear and rears to the front. For the 4WD configuration, it is dependent upon how much 4WD driving is actually performed, whether it's controlled via mechanical/computerized devices or in vehicle controls, the recommendation will likely be found in the Owner/Operator manual or can be obtained by speaking to the manufacturer or dealership.

Current thinking stresses the desirability of keeping the best tires on the rear wheels of the vehicle, whether it is front, or rear wheel drive. The reason for this is that if the rear wheels lose grip before the front ones, an oversteer condition will occur, which is harder to control than the corresponding understeer which will happen if a front wheel is lost. This is also the case if a tire blows out, so the intuitive belief that the front steering/driving tires need to be the best quality is not actually the case.

In some cases (for example, BMW), automobile manufacturers may recommend performing no tire rotation at all. Additionally, some vehicles are designed (or retrofitted) with front and rear wheels of different sizes and unidirectional rotation treads, making rotation impossible.

## External links

- Goodyear recommendations with regard to tire rotation mileage [1]
- Tire rotation patterns by Pirelli [2]

# Oil sludge

## Oil sludge

**Oil sludge** or **black sludge** is a solid or gel in motor oil caused by the oil gelling or solidifying, usually at temperatures lower than 100 degrees Celsius.

Oil sludge can be a major contributor to internal combustion engine problems, and can require the engine to be replaced, if the damage is severe. Sludge is usually caused by the presence of water in the oil, and can accumulate with use. Ways to minimize sludge production and accumulation includes performing frequent oil changes, performing mechanized engine flushing, or de-sludging, or using synthetic oil, and following the manufacturer's engine maintenance routine.

### External links

- A technical article about oil sludge, with photos [1]

# Auto detailing

## Auto detailing

**Auto detailing** (UK: **Car valeting**), is the performance of an extremely thorough cleaning, polishing and waxing of an automobile, both inside and out, to produce a show-quality level of detail. Besides improving appearance, detailing helps to preserve resale value of a car.

## Components of detailing

### Exterior detailing

**Exterior detailing** involves cleaning and bringing a shine to the car's paint, chrome trim, windows, wheels, and tires. Different detailers use different products to do this, including detergents, detail clay, waxes, polishes, and a variety of applicators and special cloths.

The three main components of exterior car detailing are **cleaning**, **polishing**, and **protecting**. Cleaning refers to removing all foreign surface particles from exterior surfaces through the use of washing and claying. A clay bar helps to clean contamination/dirt from within the clearcoat that cannot be removed through weekly washing. Clearcoat contamination can come from industrial fallout, air particles, dirt particles, tar, and animal droppings. Correcting refers to using mechanical polishes by hand or with a machine and specific polishing pads that remove a fine layer of clearcoat from a vehicle to remove fine scratches and swirls from a paint surface produced from improper washing or drying technique. Protecting involves the application of a protective material (in liquid or paste form) that prevents foreign matter from adhering to the surface of the vehicle, including water, bugs splatter, tar, and dirt. Waxes and sealants provide this barrier against the elements.

### Interior detailing

**Interior detailing** involves cleaning the passenger compartment of the car. Vacuuming is standard, and steam cleaning, liquid cleaners, and brushes may be used to remove stains on upholstery. Some nonporous surfaces may also be polished.

Advertisers have claimed that environmentally friendly car valeting can enable people to reduce their carbon footprint.

## engine detailing

Some detailers may offer **engine detailing**, in which steam, high pressure water, degreasers and all-purpose cleaners are used to clean under the hood of the car.

Detailing does not include body work, painting, mechanical or upholstery repair.

# See also

- Automotive restoration

# User guide

## User guide

A **user guide** or **user's guide**, also commonly known as a **manual**, is a technical communication document intended to give assistance to people using a particular system. It is usually written by a technical writer, although user guides are written by programmers, product or project managers, or other technical staff, particularly in smaller companies.

User guides are most commonly associated with electronic goods, computer hardware and software.

Most user guides contain both a written guide and the associated images. In the case of computer applications, it is usual to include screenshots of how the program should look, and hardware manuals often include clear, simplified diagrams. The language used is matched to the intended audience, with jargon kept to a minimum or explained thoroughly.

### Contents of a user manual

The sections of a user manual often include:

* A cover page
* A title page and copyright page
* A preface, containing details of related documents and information on how to navigate the user guide
* A contents page
* A guide on how to use at least the main functions of the system
* A troubleshooting section detailing possible errors or problems that may occur, along with how to fix them
* A FAQ (Frequently Asked Questions)
* Where to find further help, and contact details
* A glossary and, for larger documents, an index

### Computer software manuals and guides

User manuals and user guides for most non-trivial software applications are book-like documents with contents similar to the above list. The *Starta User Manual* is a good example of this type of document. Some documents have a more fluid structure with many internal links. The *Google Earth User Guide* is an example of this format. The term *guide* is often applied to a document that addresses a specific aspect of a software product. Some usages are *Installation Guide*, *Getting Started Guide*, and various *How to* guides. An example is the *Picasa Getting Started Guide*.

In some business software applications, where groups of users have access to only a sub-set of the application's full functionality, a user guide may be prepared for each group. An example of this approach is the *Autodesk Topobase 2010 Help* document, which contains separate *Administrator Guides*, *User Guides*, and a *Developer's Guide*. These guides are a valuable tool for *On-the-job* training.

## See also

- Release notes
- Moe book
- Technical writer
- Manual page (Unix)
- Instruction manual (gaming)
- Reference card

# Car wash

## Car wash

A **car wash** or **auto wash** is a facility used to clean the exterior and, in some cases, the interior of motor vehicles.

## Categories

While there are many different types of car washes, most fall into the following categories:

- Hand car wash facilities, where the vehicle is washed by employees.
- Self-service facilities, which are generally coin-operated, where the customer does the washing, including "jet washing".
- In-bay automatics, which consist of an automatic machine that rolls back and forth over a stationary vehicle - often seen at filling stations and stand-alone wash sites.
- Tunnel washes, which use a conveyor to move the vehicle through a series of fixed cleaning mechanisms.
- Chemical car wash, also known as waterless car wash, uses chemicals to wash and polish car surface. Known to have originated from Australia and has been well-received as an eco-friendly car wash method around the world, that saves water.

Mechanized car washes, especially those with brushes, were once avoided by some meticulous car owners because of the risk of damaging the finish. Paint finishes have improved as have car washing processes, and this perception of vehicle damage is much less today. However, it was the motive behind the rise of facilities utilizing "brushless" (cloth) and "touch-free" (high-pressure water) equipment, as well as "foam" washing wheels made of closed cell foam.

In today's modern car wash facilities, whether tunnel automatic, in-bay automatic or self-serve, soaps and other cleaning solutions used are based on milder acids and alkalies designed to loosen and eliminate dirt and grime. This is in contrast to earlier times, when hydrofluoric acid, a hazardous chemical, was commonly used as a cleaning agent in the industry by some operators. There has been a strong move in the industry to shift to safer cleaning solutions. Most car wash facilities are required by law to treat and/or reuse their water and may be required to maintain waste-water discharge permits, in contrast to unregulated facilities or even driveway washing where waste-water can end up in the storm drain and, eventually, in streams, rivers and lakes.

# Self-serve car wash

A simple and automated type of car wash that is typically coin-operated or token-operated self-service system. Newer self-service car washes offer the ability to pay with credit cards. The vehicle is parked inside a large bay that is equipped with a trigger gun and wand (sprayer) and a scrub foam-brush. When customers insert coins or tokens into the controller, they can choose options such as soap, tire cleaner, wax or rinse all dispensed from the sprayer, or scrub the vehicle with the foam-brush. The number of coins or tokens inserted determines the amount of time customers have to operate the equipment, however in most instances, a

A multi-bay self-service car wash, with an automatic "touchless" bay at the far left and manual bays on the right.

minimum number of coins are necessary to start the equipment. These facilities are often equipped with separate vacuum stations that allow customers to clean the upholstery and rugs inside their cars. Some self-service car washes offer hand-held dryers, a somewhat new feature.

# Automatic car wash

Rotating brushes inside a conveyor car-wash.

The first conveyorized automatic car washes appeared in the late 1930s. Conveyorized automatic car washes consist of tunnel-like buildings into which customers (or attendants) drive. Some car washes have their customers pay through a computerized *POS*, or point of sale unit, also known as an "automatic cashier", which may take the place of a human greeter. The mechanism inputs the wash PLU into a master computer or a tunnel controller automatically. When the sale is automated, after paying the car is put into a line-up often called the stack or queue. The stack moves sequentially, so the wash knows what each car purchased. After pulling up to the tunnel entrance, an attendant usually guides the customer onto the track or conveyor. At some washes, both tires will pass over a tire sensor, and the system will send several rollers. The tire sensor lets the wash know where the wheels are and how far apart they are. On other systems the employee may guide the customer on and hit a 'Send Car' button on the tunnel controller, to manually send the rollers which push the car through.

When the customer is on the conveyor, the attendant (or signage) will instruct the customer to put the vehicle into neutral, release all brakes, and refrain from steering. Failure to do so can cause an accident on the conveyor. The rollers come up behind the tires, pushing the car through a detector, which measures vehicle length, allowing the controller to tailor the wash to each individual vehicle. The equipment frame, or arches, vary in number and type. A good car wash makes use of many different pieces of equipment and stages of chemical application to thoroughly clean the vehicle.

The carwash will generally start cleaning with pre-soaks applied through special arches. They may apply a lower pH (mild acid) followed by a higher pH (mild alkali), or the order may be reversed depending on chemical suppliers and formula used. Chemical formulas and concentrations will also vary based upon seasonal dirt and film on vehicles, as well as exterior temperature, and other factors. Chemical dilution and application works in combination with removal systems based on either high pressure water, friction, or a combination of both. Chemical substances, while they are industrial strength, are not used in harmful concentrations since car washes are designed not to harm a vehicle's components or finish.

The customer next encounters tire and wheel nozzles, which the industry calls CTAs (Chemical Tire Applicators). These will apply specialized formulations, which remove brake dust and build up from the surface of the wheels and tires. The next arch will often be wraparounds, usually made of a soft cloth, or closed cell foam material. These wraparounds should rub the front bumper and, after washing the sides, will follow across the rear of the vehicle cleaning the rear including the license plate area. Past the first wraps or entrance wraps may be a tire brush that will scrub the tires and wheels. This low piece is often located beneath a mitter (the hanging ribbon-like curtains of cloth that move front to back or side to side) or top wheels. There may also be rocker panel washers which are shorter in size (ranging in size from 18 inches [45 cm] up to 63 inches [160 cm] tall) that clean the lower parts of the vehicle. Most rocker brushes house the motor below the brush hub so they don't inhibit cloth movement and allow the brush to be mounted under a support frame or below a mitter. Some car washes have multiple mitters, or a combination of mitters *and* top brushes.

Typical "tunnel" car wash view from the inside

After the mitter or top brush(es) the car may pass through a second set of wraparounds. This may also be where high pressure water streams are used to clean difficult to reach parts of the vehicle. The car generally passes over an under carriage wash and/or has high pressure nozzles pointed at it from various positions. Next may be a tire spinner, high pressure nozzles angled specifically to clean wheels and tires. After the several wash stations the vehicle may go through triple foamers, usually red, blue, and yellow, although colors can be customized with higher end chemical suppliers. The triple foam process includes special cleaners as well as some protective paint sealant.

Some washes have multiple rinse stages, usually offering a protectant as an option.

Protectants vary by manufacturer. Near the rinse is where a tire shining machine is often installed, which is designed to apply silicone tire dressing to the tires. This application makes the tires look good (new, and glossy) and preserves the rubber. Next the vehicle is treated with a drying agent and a final rinse. Many carwashes utilize a "spot free" rinse of soft water that has been filtered of chlorine and sent through semi permeable membranes to produce highly purified water that will not leave spots. After using spot free water, the vehicle is finished with forced air drying, in some cases utilizing heat to produce a very dry car.

Older automatic washes-a majority of which were built prior to 1980-used to use brushes with soft nylon bristles, which tended to leave a nylon deposit in the shape of a bristle, called brushmarks, on the vehicle's paint. Many brushes in the US are now either cloth (which is not harmful to a car's finish, as long as it is flushed with plenty of water to remove the grit from previous washes), or a closed cell foam brush, which does not hold dirt or water, thus is far less likely to harm any painted finish, and can, in fact, provide a gentle polishing effect to leave the paint much shinier. In order to avoid paint

A touchless car wash

marking issues, "touchless" or "no-touch" car washes were developed. This means the car is washed with high water pressure instead of brushes. There is no contact with friction so the chance of any damage is less, however the actual cleaning, or removal of film from the paint, is nearly impossible with no touch systems.

At "full-service" car washes, the exterior of the car is washed mechanically with conveyorized equipment, or in some cases by hand, with attendants available to dry the car manually, and to clean the interior (normally consisting of cleaning the windows, wiping the front and side dashes, and vacuuming the carpet and upholstery). Many full service car washes also provide "detailing" services, which may include polishing and waxing the car's exterior by hand or machine, shampooing and steaming interiors, and other services to provide thorough cleaning and protection to the car.

# Bikini car wash

Bikini car washes are a summer event that occurs, usually for two purposes:

New Zealand Bikini car wash

- It may be a fund raiser for a school or a sport association or another youth organization or charity. Typically, females in bikinis bring in odors by standing on a roadside with colorful cardboard signs or posters, and the cars are washed by their classmates in a nearby parking lot.
- Depending on the organization responsible, as well as the local laws, a variation of the bikini car wash sometimes occurs, in which the girls will wash the car topless, usually for an extra fee. This type of carwash is not found in the US as part of any legitimate charitable or fundraising event.
- There are also commercial bikini car washes, where bikini-clad girls actually wash the cars for a fee and the entertainment of the drivers. Hooters restaurants usually have bikini car washes in the summer to attract customers.

# Environmental factors

The primary environmental considerations for car washing are:

- Use of water and energy resources;
- Contamination of surface waters;
- Contamination of soil and groundwater.

Use of water supplies and energy are self-evident, since car washes are users of such resources. The professional car wash industry has made great strides in reducing its environmental footprint, a trend that will continue to accelerate due to regulation and consumer demand. Many car washes already use water reclamation systems to significantly reduce water usage and a variety of energy usage reduction technologies. These systems may be mandatory where water restrictions are in place.

Contamination of surface waters arises from the rinseate discharging to storm drains, which in turn most commonly drain to rivers and lakes. Chief pollutants in such wash-water include phosphates; oil and grease; and lead. This is almost exclusively an issue for home/driveway washing, and parking lot style charity washes. Professional carwashing is a "non-point source" of discharge that has the ability to capture these contaminants and have them undergo treatment before being released into sanitary systems. (Water and contaminants that enter storm water drains does not undergo treatment, and is released directly into rivers, lakes and streams.)

Soil contamination is sometimes related to such surface runoff, but more importantly is associated with soil contamination from underground fuel tanks or auto servicing operations which commonly are ancillary uses of car wash sites — but not an issue for car washing itself.

For these reasons, some state and local environmental groups (the most notable being the New Jersey Department of Environmental Protection) have begun campaigns to encourage consumers to use professional car washes as opposed to driveway washing, including moving charity car wash fund raisers from parking lots to professional car washes.

## See also

- Auto detailing
- Jetwash

## External links

- How Car Washes Work [1] at HowStuffWorks
- International Carwash Association [2]
- Carwash Database [3]
- Steam Car Wash System / SJE Corporation [4]
- the first steam car wash machine / Steamjet Syetems [5]

# Grease gun (tool)

## Grease gun (tool)

A **grease gun** is a common workshop and garage tool used for lubrication. The purpose of the grease gun is to apply lubricant through an aperture to a specific point, usually on a grease fitting. The channels behind the grease nipple lead to where the lubrication is needed. The aperture may be of a type that fits closely with a receiving aperture on any number of mechanical devices. The close fitting of the apertures ensures that lubricant is applied only where needed. There are three types of grease gun:

1. Hand-powered, where the grease is forced from the aperture by back-pressure built up by hand cranking the trigger mechanism of the gun, which applies pressure to a spring mechanism behind the lubricant, thus forcing grease through the aperture.
2. Hand-powered, where there is no trigger mechanism, and the grease is forced through the aperture by the back-pressure built up by pushing on the butt of the grease gun, which slides a piston through the body of the tool, pumping grease out of the aperture.

A grease gun (pneumatic)

The grease gun is charged or loaded with any of the various types of lubricants, but usually a thicker heavier type of grease is used.

It was a close resemblance to contemporary hand-powered grease guns that gave the nickname to the World War II-era M3 submachine gun.

## See also

• Grease gun injury

# Back-fire

## Back-fire

*For other meanings of the term see backfire.*

A **Back-fire** or **backfire** is an explosion produced by a running internal combustion engine that occurs in the intake or exhaust system rather than inside the combustion chamber. The same term is used when unburned fuel or hydrocarbons are ignited somewhere in the exhaust system. A visible flame may momentarily shoot out of the exhaust pipe. Either condition causes an objectionable popping noise, together with possible loss of power and forward motion. A backfire is a separate phenomenon from the fire produced by Top Fuel dragsters.

Backfiring racing motorcycle

Also, an explosion in the inlet manifold, carburetor/throttle body, or air cleaner of an internal combustion engine can occur when the intake valves are not shut prior to fuel combustion.

The term was derived from experiences with early unreliable firearms or ammunition, in which the explosive force was directed out the breech instead of the muzzle. From this came the use of the word "backfire" as a verb to indicate something that produces an unintended, unexpected, and undesired result.

## Explanation

Backfire in an automobile engine typically results from various malfunctions related to the air to fuel ratio. Backfiring can occur in carbureted engines that are running lean where the air-fuel mixture has insufficient fuel and whenever the timing is too advanced. As the engine runs leaner or if there is less time for the fuel to burn in the combustion chamber, there is a tendency for incomplete combustion. The condition that causes this is a misfire. The result of a misfire or incomplete combustion is that unburned fuel or flammable hydrocarbons are delivered to the exhaust manifold where it may ignite unpredictably. Another backfire situation occurs when the engine is running rich (with excess fuel) and there is incomplete combustion during the Otto cycle, with similar results.

Popularly the term is used to describe a sharp report produced by almost any type of engine. However, among engine professionals, "afterfire" is the term used to describe ignition of fuel within the engine exhaust system and "backfire" is the term used to describe this same process taking place in the induction system, primarily in internal combustion engines. The separate terms are useful when troubleshooting running problems.

When starting an engine, timing that is too advanced will fire the spark plug before the intake valve is closed. The flame front will travel back in to the intake manifold, igniting all of that air and fuel as well. The resulting explosion then travels out of the carburetor and air cleaner. A common air filter will allow the gases to escape, but will block the flame front. On many small marine engines, no air filter is used, but a screen is placed over the intake of the carburetor as a flame arrestor to prevent these flames from escaping the intake, and potentially igniting fuel, or fuel vapors in the enclosed sump or bilge of the boat and causing a fire or explosion. Improperly adjusted carburetors that create a lean condition during acceleration can cause the air fuel mixture to burn so slowly, that combustion is still taking place during the exhaust stroke, and even when the intake valve opens. The flame front can then travel up the intake and cause a backfire. In this situation it is conceivable that there is a backfire occurring in the intake manifold and exhaust manifold simultaneously.

# Causes

Exhaust system backfires occur in engines that have an emission system malfunction, like an air injection system diverter valve problem, an exhaust leak, or when the catalytic converter has been removed. In some high-performance vehicles, when a driver shifts up and lets off the accelerator, the engine has a moment of running rich. This causes an incomplete burn which causes the fumes to explode in the exhaust system along with an audible clacking sound. However this condition is a result of working smog equipment, and is unlikely to cause any damage.

A fuel injected engine may backfire if an intake leak is present (causing the engine to run lean), or a fuel injection component such as an air-flow sensor is defective.

Common causes of backfires are:

- Poor or unregulated engine timing is often a cause of intake backfires, but can also be responsible for exhaust backfires
- Improper wiring in the ignition can also lead to timing issues and backfires
- Low fuel pressure, clogged fuel filters, and weak fuel pumps could cause a severe lean air-to-fuel ratio during fuel injection
- Missing or damaged catalytic converter can result in backfires out the tailpipe

## Applications

With older engine designs, backfiring can be common or unavoidable. Backfire is rare in modern vehicles with fuel-injection and computer-controlled fuel mixtures.

In drag racing, backfires in the intake usually result in the complete destruction of the intake manifold, carburetors, supercharger, and sometimes engine.

Cars with sports exhausts (both factory-fitted and aftermarket) are much more likely to backfire. In some circumstances the backfire is seen as an additional perk of the car. The TVR Cerbera is an example of a car with factory-fitted sports exhausts which produce frequent backfires on engine braking.

## Purposely made

Tanks and naval ships may use the injection of fuel or special "fog oil" into exhaust tract to create smoke screens. Rather than burning, the oil normally evaporates and re-condenses at a particular droplet size, but under abnormal conditions it may catch fire or even produce a fuel-air explosion.

Cars extensively modified for visual appearance and not road use (stunts, ads, movies etc.) may be fitted with gasoline injectors in their exhaust systems, or even with small flamethrowers completely separate from the actual exhaust.

## See also

- Dieseling, an after-run condition in which an engine continues to run without the spark plugs firing
- Ignition timing
- Valve timing

# Cold inflation pressure

## Cold inflation pressure

**Cold inflation pressure** is the inflation pressure of tires before the car is driven and the tires warmed up. Recommended cold inflation pressure is displayed on the owner's manual and on the placard (or sticker) attached to the vehicle door edge, pillar, glovebox door or fuel filler flap. Drivers concerned about gas mileage are encouraged to make sure their tires are adequately inflated, as suboptimal tire pressure can greatly reduce fuel economy.

Tire pressure is measured in psi, bar or kilopascal.

### See also

- Direct TPMS
- Tire-pressure gauge
- Tire-pressure monitoring system

# Haynes Manual

## Haynes Manual

The **Haynes Owner's Workshop Manuals** (commonly known as simply **Haynes Manuals**) are a series of practical manuals from the Haynes Publishing Group aimed at both DIY enthusiasts and professional garage mechanics. The series primarily focuses upon the maintenance and repair of automotive vehicles, covering a wide range of makes and models (300 models of car and 130 models of motorcycle), but it also includes manuals in the same style for domestic appliances and personal computers, digital photography and model railways, men and babies, sex, and women. The last four were made slightly tongue in cheek, but have proved very popular.

A Haynes manual based on the various Starships *Enterprise* from the various *Star Trek* television series and motion pictures is in development for release in September 2010.

## History

Many Haynes Manuals bear a cover illustration of a stripped down technical drawing of the vehicle, hand-drawn by Terry Davey, and they bear his signature.

## Strip down and rebuild

## For professionals

Manuals for garage professionals include books such as the *Automotive Diesel Engine Service Guide*, the *Automotive Air Conditioning TechBook*, *Citroën and Peugeot Engine Management Systems*, and two *Engine Management and Fuel Injection Systems Pin Tables and Wiring Diagrams TechBook* volumes.

## Distribution

Haynes manuals are published in 15 languages: English (including British, American and Australian variants), French, Swedish, Chinese, Japanese, German, Czech, Finnish, Polish, Bulgarian, Hebrew, Greek, Danish, Spanish (including American Spanish versions), and Russian.

## Location

The company is based in Sparkford, a village near Yeovil in Somerset, England. The Haynes International Motor Museum, the largest motor museum in the UK, is also in Yeovil, and it is home to a large collection of both classic and modern cars, and many rarities.

## Authorship

Haynes manuals are written by a pair of authors, and take between 20 and 30 man-weeks. A car or motorcycle is bought at the beginning of the project and sold at the end. Although the workshop phase of the project usually lasts for roughly four weeks, the vehicle is usually retained for a couple of months to ensure it is functioning correctly.

## Tooling

## Manufacturers

## See also

- Chilton Publishing Company
- Clymer repair manual
- Cyclepedia Repair Manuals
- how-to

## External links

- Haynes web site [1]

# Wheel alignment

## Wheel alignment

**Wheel alignment** is part of standard automobile maintenance that consists of adjusting the angles of the wheels so that they are set to the car maker's specification. The purpose of these adjustments is to reduce tire wear, and to ensure that vehicle travel is straight and true (without "pulling" to one side). Alignment angles can also be altered beyond the maker's specifications to obtain a specific handling characteristic. Motorsport and off-road applications may call for angles to be adjusted well beyond "normal" for a variety of reasons.

### Primary angles

The primary angles are the basic angle alignment of the wheels relative to each other and to the car body. These adjustments are the camber, caster and toe. On some cars, not all of these can be adjusted on every wheel.

These three parameters can be further categorized into front and rear, so summarily the parameters are:

- Front: Caster (right& left)
- Front: Camber (right & left)
- Front: Toe (left, right & total)
- Rear: Camber (left & right)
- Rear: Toe (left, right & total)
- Rear: Thrust angle

### Secondary angles

The secondary angles include numerous other adjustments, such as:

- SAI (left & right)
- Included angle (left & right)
- Toe out on turns (left & right)
- Maximum Turns (left & right)
- Toe curve change (left & right)
- Track width difference
- Wheel base difference
- Front ride height (left & right)

- Rear ride height (left & right)
- Frame angle

Setback (front & rear) is often referred as a wheel alignment angle. However setback simply exists because of the measuring system and does not have any specification from car manufacturers.

## Measurement

A camera unit (sometimes called a "head") is attached to a specially designed clamp which holds on to a wheel. There are usually four camera units in a wheel alignment system (a camera unit for each wheel). The camera units communicate their physical positioning with respect to other camera units to a central computer which calculates and displays how much the camber, toe and caster are misaligned.

Often with alignment equipment, these "heads" can be a large precision reflector. In this case, the alignment "tower" contains the cameras as well as arrays of LEDs. This system flashes one array of LEDs for each reflector whilst a camera centrally located in the LED array "looks for" an image of the reflectors patterned face. These cameras perform the same function as the other style of alignment equipment, yet alleviate numerous issues prone to relocating a heavy precision camera assembly on each vehicle serviced.

## See also

- Car handling
- Car maintenance
- Auto mechanic
- Tire rotation
- ASE

## External links

- Bee Line Company [1] Leading Manufacturer of Heavy Duty Alignment Equipment
- A short course on alignment [2]
- How Truck Alignments Affect Fuel Mileage [3]

# Auto mechanic

## Auto mechanic

An **auto mechanic** (or **car mechanic** in British English and **motor mechanic** in Australian English) is a mechanic who specializes in automobile maintenance, repair, and sometimes modification. An auto mechanic may be knowledgeable in working on all parts of a variety of car makes or may specialize either in a specific area or in a specific make of car. In repairing cars, their main role is to diagnose the problem accurately and quickly. They often have to quote prices for their customers before commencing work or after partial disassembly for inspection. The mechanic uses both electronic

A mechanic working on the differential of a car

means of gathering data as well as their senses. Their job may involve the repair of a specific part or the replacement of one or more parts as assemblies.

### Overview

Basic vehicle maintenance is a fundamental part of a mechanic's work in some countries, while in others they are consulted only when a vehicle is already showing signs of malfunction. Preventative maintenance is also a fundamental part of a mechanic's job, but this is not possible in the case of vehicles that are not regularly maintained by a mechanic. One misunderstood aspect of preventative maintenance is *scheduled replacement* of various parts, which occurs before failure to avoid far more expensive damage. Because this means that parts are replaced before any problem is observed, many vehicle owners will not understand why the expense is necessary. The salary depends on the education.

With the rapid advancement in technology, the mechanic's job has evolved from being purely mechanical to including electronic technology. Because vehicles today possess complex computer and electronic systems, mechanics need to have a broader base of knowledge than in the past. Lately, the term "auto mechanic" is being used less and less frequently and is being replaced by the euphemistic title "automotive service technician". Fading quickly is the day of the 'shade tree mechanic', who needed little knowledge of today's computerized systems.

Due to the increasingly labyrinthine nature of the technology that is now incorporated into automobiles, most automobile dealerships now provide sophisticated diagnostic computers to each technician, without which they may be not be able to diagnose or repair electronic issues in modern vehicles. The TIEC system is most popular in Northern England. There are things that mechanics can still do with out the use of scanners etc but manufacturers are incorporating more and more electronics into all systems. That will make the mechanic a thing of the past; only technicians with extensive training and special tools will be able to fix those systems.

# Education

## Australia

In Australia, an apprentice works under one or more qualified mechanics for a period of four years. During that time, they attend a Technical and Further Education (TAFE) college one day per week for three years. In some states, mechanics are required to be trade qualified and hold a tradesman's certificate to work as a mechanic, and the workshop in which they work is required to have a workshop license. In other states, no such licensing is required at this time.

## USA

In the United States, community colleges and private car training schools offer training for those interested in pursuing competencies as an automotive mechanic/technician. High schools may have programs also. "Though employers seem to prefer postsecondary training". A few of the aspects usually taught those studying for this career are: powertrain repair and diagnosis, emissions, and suspension. Courses can include engine repair, electrical systems, brake systems, manual and automatic transmissions, suspension and steering, heating and air conditioning, basic fuel and ignition systems, and emissions. The National Automotive Technicians Education Foundation (NATEF) is responsible for evaluating technician training programs against standards developed by the automotive industry. NATEF certifies programs in four different categories: automotive, auto body, trucks (diesel technology) and alternative fuels. A list of NATEF schools is available at the ASE website through the NATEF link. Postsecondary education can consist of either one or more cerfifcates, or 1 - 2 years of training. Typically WyoTech.

Some mechanics are ASE certified, which is a standardized method of testing skill level. For most of the country, it is not required by law for a mechanic to be certified, some companies only hire or promote employees who have passed ASE tests. The technology used in automobiles changes very rapidly and the mechanic must be prepared to learn these new technologies and systems. The auto mechanic has a physically demanding job, often exposed to temperature extremes and well as lifting heavy objects and staying in uncomfortable positions for extended periods as well as exposure to gasoline, asbestos, and other toxic chemicals.

## UK

In the UK the mechanic or technician is trained to diagnose and repair the entire vehicle, in other countries they have specialist "shops" for example wheels and tyres, or brakes but in the UK the mechanic repairs all of these systems. Education can start at 14 with the new Diploma and then progress until level three certificates are obtained, this is done usually on an apprenticeship scheme the first level been the foundation apprenticeship where they must achieve a level II technical certificate (the understanding) and a leve II NVQ (the practical part of the job) this is assessed by a competent, qualified assessor, they then progress to the advanced apprenticeship which the qualifications are set at level III, the mechanic will then tend to be given easy jobs to build up experience over a period of time. Once the mechanic has achieved level III they can apply to be ATA tested, this is a scheme similar to the ASE scheme where they are assessed and registered for 5 yrs as certified, then after 5 yrs they renew this registration by completing a set of practical and theory tests, the idea behind this scheme is to eliminate poor practice

# Related careers

A mechanic may opt to engage in other careers related to his field. Teaching of automotive trade courses, for example, is almost entirely carried out by qualified mechanics in many countries.

There are several other trade qualifications for working on motor vehicles, including *panel beater*, *spray painter*, *body builder* and *motorcycle mechanic*. In some countries, these are separate trade courses, but a qualified tradesman from one can change to working as another. This usually requires that they work under another tradesman in much the same way as an apprentice.

Auto body repair involves less work with oily and greasy parts of vehicles, but involves exposure to particulate dust from sanding bodywork and potentially toxic chemical fumes from paint and related products. Salespeople and dealers often also need to acquire an in-depth knowledge of cars, and some mechanics are successful in these roles because of their knowledge.

In a Car Dealership a Mechanic may also be assigned in Parts Department as a Parts Counter Salesman because of their wide knowledge and familiarity of vehicle parts. Parts Counter Salesman Facilitates selling, marketing, inventory and issuance of vehicle parts, accessories and lubricants to over the counter clients and service technicians.

A Mechanic may also be assigned in Tool Room as a Tool Keeper because of their expertise and knowledge about tools, gadgets to be used in overhauling, diagnosing, troubleshooting, testing the vehicles mechanical, electrical and electronic trouble.

A Mechanic may also be promoted as a Service Advisor assigned in service reception entertaining walk-in or by appointment customers who wish their vehicle to be diagnosed, perform quality service check-up and estimate cost of damage.

A Mechanic may also be a consultant of automotive shop owners and engage in Sales as a Technical Sales Representative selling automotive hardware like tools, screw, chemicals and other engineering and industrial product which supplies and caters different 5 star car dealership, service center, auto supply, car wash shop and car accessories shop because of their knowledge about the products where, when, how they are going to used it appropriately in a specific vehicle.

A Mechanic may also venture into business as entrepreneur putting up his own automotive service center/shop or auto supply and accessories since he already have a wide knowledge of day to day operations of a service center and already builds a network of customers and parts supplier.

A Mechanic may also be a sales or service trainer in a car dealership teaching basic automotive fundamentals in sales or service department because of their knowledge about principles and function of every parts, accessories and latest specification of the vehicle.

There is a segment of auto repair that is getting very popular. The mobile mechanic. There are many regular mechanics that are opting to instead of opening an expensive regular shop they go with the less expensive mobile shop route. There are still overhead expenses but they are less. But also the amount of cars fixed per week are less too. The convenience of a mobile mechanic should make them more expensive but usually they aren't. Actually most are even less than dealers and regular shops. So they are really an option to consider when needing a car repair.

## Pit crews

Pit crews for motor racing are a specialized form of work undertaken by some mechanics. It is sometimes portrayed as glamorous in movies and television and is considered prestigious in some parts of the automotive industry. Working in a pit crew in professional racing circuits is dangerous and very stressful work but usually pays well. This work is sometimes perceived as being difficult to come by because of the skill levels required. Pit crews have to be smart and can fix a car fast and well. Some of the Pit Crew mechanics background are former service technician of a road car in a dealership. Every four years car manufacturers conduct a service technician competition single and double and there are different categories like light, medium repair and general job within a certain time to beat. As a service technician champion they used this credential and experience as a stepping stone in order for them to be qualified as a pit crew mechanic in F1, GP2, IIS(Izod Indycar Series) , NASCAR, A1GP, WRC and including other racing competitions.

## Aircraft

A mechanic who works on aircraft is called a Aircraft Maintenance Technician (or Aviation mechanic in the United States). The skill set and techniques are very similar, especially for those working with general aviation aircraft.

## External links

- Princeton Review, Career Profiles [1]
- National Automotive Technicians Education Foundation [2]
- Automotive Youth Educational Systems [3]
- Canadian Automotive Repair and Service (CARS) Council [4]

# Cutting compound

## Cutting compound

**Cutting compound** consists of an abrasive suspended in a paste. Like most abrasives, it comes in various grit sizes dependent upon how much matter is to be removed. It is used on automotive paintwork to cut through (abrade) oxidised paint or to polish out scratches in the paintwork. The oxidised paint is duller than fresh paint and the cutting compound is used to expose this fresher surface. Modern automotive painting often includes a thin, transparent protective coating on which cutting compound should not be used. Cutting is not something that should necessarily be done often as it will eventually strip all the paint from the surface, which both is less appealing and offers less chemical resistance. Waxing to protect the newly exposed surface is an important part of maintenance.

# Full service

## Full service

**Full service** is a term that has many different uses. In general the term implies that the customer will receive as much service as is reasonably possible.

### Gas station

A full service gas station indicates that besides pumping your fuel, the attendant will also wash your windows and check your vehicle's fluids. While obsolete in many places, it is legally mandated in the U.S. states of New Jersey and Oregon.

### Hotels

Full availability of requisite standardized industry amenities; not limited to, but including the following: on-premise restaurants, room service, business center, concierge, fitness center, banquet halls, various room type selection (suites, etc.)

### Car wash

A full service car wash indicates that in addition to simple washing your vehicle, the attendants will wash the interior glass, vacuum the interior and clean the seats.

### Radio

Main article: Full service (radio format)

A full service radio format consists of a mixture of news, music and talk shows, aimed toward a wide audience.

### Paid sexual service

Full service is usually used by a massage parlour or outcall service to indicate that the individuals working as adult service providers will provide sexual intercourse. The 2009 documentary *Happy Endings?* filmed in Asian massage parlors in Rhode Island where prostitution was legal until 2009 covers the distinction between "full service" and "rub n tug" massage parlors.

# Rest area

A full service rest area is one that offers a gas station, food, rest rooms and other amenities for travelers.

# Engineering

A full service engineering firm indicates that all engineering disciplines and staff required to construct a building or complete a building project are housed within the same company. The included disciplines are: Civil Engineering, Structural Engineering, Mechanical Engineering, Electrical Engineering and Plumbing Engineering.

# Food service

A full service restaurant is used to describe a facility with table service.

# See also

• Full Service Network

# Automotive restoration

## Automotive restoration

**Automobile restoration** is the process of repairing all aspects and parts of a car to return it to the exact condition it was in when it was first offered for sale.

A complete restoration includes not only repair of the parts that can be seen – the body, the trim, the chrome, the wheels, the dash board and accessories and the passenger's compartment – but the parts that are not necessarily visible or otherwise evident, including the engine and the engine compartment, the trunk, the frame, the driveline, and all ancillary parts like the brakes, accessories, engine cooling

Restored 1949 VW Bug

system, electrical system, etc. Besides repairs done to correct obvious problems, repairs are also done for cosmetic reasons. For example, even if a wheel is covered by a hub cap and not seen, and is structurally sound, it should have the tire unmounted, then any required repairs such as rust removal, straightening, priming and painting.

Restoration is sometimes confused with the term "restomod." A restomod places some portions of the car as they were when the car was first offered for sale, and changes(updates) others. If any part of the car is not as it was first offered for sale, the car has been "restomodded," and not restored. A restoration puts a car in the same condition as when it was first offered for sale.

### Dissasembly

A complete auto restoration could include total removal of the body, engine, driveline components and related parts from the car, total disassembly, cleaning and repairing of each of the major parts and its components, replacing broken, damaged or worn parts and complete re-assembly and testing. As part of the restoration, each part must be thoroughly examined, cleaned and repaired, or if repair of the individual part would be too costly, replaced (assuming correct, quality parts are available) as necessary to return the entire automobile to "as first sold" condition.

All of the parts showing wear or damage that were originally painted are typically stripped of old paint, with any rust or rust related damage repaired, dents and ripples removed and then the metal refinished, primed and painted with colors to match the original factory colors. Wooden parts should go through the same meticulous inspection and repair process with reglueing, replacement of rotted or termite-damaged wood, sealing and refinishing to match the factory specifications. Chrome and trim may require stripping and repair/refinishing. Fasteners with tool marks, damaged threads, or corrosion need re-plating or replacement-unless the car was originally sold that way. The frame must be thoroughly cleaned and repaired if necessary. Often sandblasting of the frame is the most expeditious method of cleaning. The frame must be properly coated to match the original.

## Interior

The interior of the car should be examined and repaired/replaced to match those that were available from the factory. The seats must be repaired before being re-upholstered and the coil springs repaired, replaced or retied. The instrument panel, or dash board contains a number of gauges, each of which have to be inspected and cleaned/repaired/replaced to be brought back to both operational and cosmetic standards of the car when it was first sold.

## Exterior

In a complete restoration, the repair and refinishing of the car's body and frame must again go through the careful inspection and subsequent repair,and recoating as necessary to bring the car to as first sold condition.

As part of the automotive restoration process, repair of the car's frame is important since in serves as the foundation for the entire car. The frame should be inspected for straightness, twisting, alignment, rust damage, and condition of the mounting points for the body, suspension, and other components. Any problems must be repaired, which can be a

Apperson: Before and After

costly process. For many popular cars, replacement frames can be purchased from parts suppliers specializing in that make of vehicle. This is often a better option than investing money into a severely damaged frame. Depending on the frame construction, mud and water can make their way inside the frame and cause rusting from the inside out, so it can be seriously weakened with little or no external sign. This, and the fact that many replacement chassis/frames are galvanised, provides sound additional reasons to consider a replacement frame.

If rust is present on a body panel, the panel was damaged by a collision, or other damage is present, there are several options for repair: fix the damaged panel (minor damage), replacement (excessively damaged panels), or cutting out and replacing a portion of the panel (moderate damage - for many makes of vintage car, small partial patch panels are available and designed to be welded into place after the damaged portions are cut out). Although, this may seem simple in principle, in practice it is highly skilled work. One of the highest skills in restoration is the use of the English Wheel or Wheeling Machine. Many panels, (especially if from different sources), may be a problem to fit together and need reshaping to fit properly. Variation in panel size and shape and 'fettling' by skilled metalworkers on the factory production line to make panels fit well, used to be common practice, especially with British and Italian sports cars. Even genuine New Old Stock factory panels may require panel beating skills to fit.

The re-installation of the repaired or renewed panels requires that the panels be trial fitted and aligned, to check their fit, that their shape 'flows' and the gaps between panels are correct. Consistent gaps are very important to a quality finish. Gapping gauges are available for this. The doors, hood, and trunk should open and close properly, and there should be no interference or rubbing. Steel or aluminium door skins and wing/fender edges can be generally be adjusted with a hammer and dolly, in extreme cases a pulsed MIG weld bead on a panel edge, that is shaped with a grinder, can be good solution. At one time it was common practice to use lead loading to achieve tight panel gaps, especially in the coachbuilding business, but also on the production line. The panels have to 'look right' together. This is a process of repeated adjustment, because the adjustment of one panel often affects the apparent fit of another. If there are multiple styling lines on the side of a car, it is generally best to align doors on the most prominent one. When you are satisfied with the panels on the car, they should be primed and painted a correct historical color for the vehicle (although this is debatable - the owner might want to have the car painted to look like a particular specialty vehicle such as a police car, or a delivery van painted to look like it would have in grandfather's company colors, etc.) Individual painting of the panels is generally the correct approach, as this will result in all parts of the panel being painted as opposed to partially re-assembling and then painting, leaving parts of the assembly that are touching or "blind" unpainted. It is useful to mark in some way, if possible, where the panels fit before removal for painting, to aid re-fitting. The separate painting approach should also result in no overspray on other parts of the since they will not be on the car at that point. It is important when re-assembling painted panels, to be aware that the paint is at its thinnest, and most easily damaged, on corners, edges, and raised styling lines, and to take extra care with them. This is also important when using ultra fine wet flatting paper before polishing, (or when using an electric polishing mop) for the best mirror like finish.

Colors and treatments applied to the panels, from the factory should be considered. A car's owner may wish to have a panel or portion of the car entirely painted when in fact it may have come from the factory with undercoating or other coating applied to one side, which may be less attractive than a smoothly finished and painted panel. In other cases, the owner might paint or plate a collection of small parts to look similar for a better appearance, when the factory might have installed these as many different colors since the factory's prime concern was function and not appearance. This makes the car a "Restomod", and not a restoration.

# Engine

The entire engine and all related systems are inspected and what ever is necessary to get them into original presale condition is done. The engine and all of the ancillary components — starter, generator/alternator, radiator, distributor, carburetor and all others — must be inspected and corrected to factory specifications. The engine itself, plus the transmission, clutch, overdrive unit and even the driveshaft must be meticulously inspected, cleaned and measured for wear. This will show up as deviation from original factory specifications. All of the parts — block, crankcase, head, transmission housing, etc.

Boss 302 engine

— should be inspected for cracks or other damage. All moving parts — pistons, crankshaft, camshaft, oil pump, bearing and bushings, flywheel, water pump and all others — must be cleaned and measured against factory specifications and, if necessary, machined or re-manufactured to bring them within specifications. The same goes for the transmission, clutch, differential and all other moving parts of the power line and drive line. All of the electrical system has to be inspected and, if it shows wear or damage, replaced. Then the entire engine/driveline will have to be reassembled, replacing all worn bearing and bushings, seals, gaskets, belts and gears.

# Reassembly

Finally, the engine/driveline has to be re-installed in the frame, the brakes, wheels and other parts re-installed, the body fitted to the frame and the entire car rechecked and tested.

Restoration of a car is a daunting task, not one to be undertaken lightly, or by the inexperienced. A full restoration can take many years and can cost tens of thousands of dollars; often, and generally, well in excess of what the finished value of the car will be. Many jobs will have to be farmed out to specialty shops; those with the special knowledge and equipment to do the job. Often a restoration once started is left unfinished and the car and parts can be purchased for a fraction of their worth. But if a person buys an unfinished project, it is imperative to be sure that all of the parts are there. Finding parts for an orphan or rare car can be near impossible.

There are different levels of automotive repair. The highest quality level, generally unobtainable for the amateur restorer, is the Concours d'Elegance level; these are cars that are frequently restomoded to a degree often beyond the quality that they were when they left the factory. There are virtually no deficiencies in the quality of the parts that were actually restored. Those parts that did not come on the car as it was first sold must have the highest level of fit and finish, and appear to have been original parts. Many Concours d'Elegance cars are not driven except for the short distances from their trailers to the show field.

Only when a car is completely placed back into the condition it was first sold in is it considered to be restored. Various aspect of a car may be repaired without the car being restored. A car that does not run can be repaired to running condition, but that simply means it will now run and does not mean that any part of the car has been restored. Automotive Restoration means that the car was put back into the condition it was first sold as. Anything else is either repair, or restomod. Between these two extremes are the vast bulk of cars that are seen as drivers, neighborhood show cars, 20-footers (they look great from 20 feet away). Many value guides offer six levels of quality, from a 'parts-only' car to a Number 1- absolutely perfect in every way.

For the amateur, or even experienced restorer, there are a great number of help sources, books and magazines (Skinned Knuckles or Practical Classics in the UK, for example) to assist with restoration of an entire car or specific parts. There are also enthusiast websites that can offer help advice and contacts for vehicle restoration.

## Gallery

1969 Shelby Mustang GT350

1958 Chevrolet Corvette roadster

Ford Model T

Interior of a 1949 VW Bug

## See also

- Antique car
- Custom car
- Hot rod
- Muscle car
- Rat rod
- Sodablasting
- Auto detailing
- Cosmetic restoration

# External links

- Tips & Tricks from the Pros at MetalShapers.Org [1] *The History of Automotive Aluminum* by Kent White

# Fuel starvation

## Fuel starvation

**Fuel starvation** and **fuel exhaustion** (sometimes referred to as **fuel depletion**) are problems that can affect internal combustion engines fuelled by either diesel, kerosene, petroleum or any other combustible liquid or gas. If no fuel is available for an engine to burn, it cannot function. All modes of transport powered by such engines can be affected by this problem, but the consequences are most significant when it occurs to aircraft in flight. The remainder of this article discusses primarily fuel starvation and exhaustion issues in aviation.

### Fuel exhaustion

There are two main ways that an engine can run out of fuel:

- **Using all of the fuel.** An engine can use all available fuel due to insufficient fuel being loaded for the planned journey or the journey time extended for too long (in the case of an aircraft, due to in-flight delays or problems). Incidents of this type involving aircraft include Air Canada Flight 143, Avianca Flight 52, and Ethiopian Airlines Flight 961.
- **Leaking.** In some cases, the fuel tank or the supply piping to the engine leaks and fuel is lost. This can cause engines to starve. Cases of this nature involving aircraft include Air Transat Flight 236.

### Fuel starvation

Fuel starvation is slightly different from fuel exhaustion, in that fuel is in the tank but there is a supply problem which either fully or partially prevents the fuel from reaching the engine. Causes may include a blocked fuel filter, problems with fuel tank selection if multiple tanks are installed, or more commonly water-contaminated fuel. Fuel has a lower specific gravity than water which means that any water in the fuel will collect in the bottom of a fuel tank. As fuel is typically drawn from the lowest part of the tank, water is delivered to the engine instead and the engine starves.

# Fuel exhaustion and starvation incidents on aircraft

Many incidents have happened on aircraft where fuel exhaustion or starvation played a role. A partial list of these incidents follows:

- On 19 June 1954, a Convair CV-240 aircraft operated by Swissair registered HR-IBW ran out of fuel over the English Channel near Folkestone. The aircraft ditched in the Channel, killing three passengers. Four crew members and two passengers were found alive after the crash.

- On 3 August 1954, a Lockheed 1049C Super Constellation of Air France registered F-BGNA was diverted to Boston after being unable to land at New York-Idlewild Airport due to bad weather. It ran out of fuel before reaching Boston and made a belly-landing in a field. There were no fatalities.

- On 21 August 1963, a Tupolev Tu-124 operated by Aeroflot registered SSSR-45021 experienced a landing gear malfunction after taking off from Tallinn Airport. On finding that the nose gear could neither be retracted nor extended, the crew diverted the flight to Leningrad where they prepared for an emergency landing by circling the city burning off fuel. While circling the city the crew made repeated attempts to get the landing gear to lock down; they possibly became over-preoccupied with this and the aircraft ran out of fuel. The crew ditched the aircraft in the Neva River. There were no fatalities.

- A British Midland Canadair C-4 Argonaut registered G-ALHG suffered a double engine failure due to a fuel tank selector problem over Stockport, England on 4 June 1967. The aircraft crashed and 72 of the 84 onboard died.

- ALM Flight 980 was a Douglas DC-9-33CF flying from John F. Kennedy International Airport in New York City to Princess Juliana International Airport in St. Maarten, in the Netherlands Antilles, on 2 May 1970. Multiple diversions due to severe weather conditions and several unsuccessful landing attempts depleted the aircraft's fuel to the point where the crew believed there was insufficient remaining to reach an alternative airport and decided to ditch the DC-9 in the Caribbean Sea. There were 23 fatalities among the 63 on board.

- United Airlines Flight 173, a Douglas DC-8-61 en route from Denver, Colorado to Portland, Oregon on 28 December 1978 experienced a landing gear indicator light malfunction while preparing to land. The aircraft continued to circle in the vicinity of Portland while the crew investigated the problem, but it ran out of fuel and crash-landed in a sparsely populated area, killing 10 and seriously injuring 24 of the 181 on board.

- On 23 July 1983, due to a chain of events and mistakes Air Canada Flight 143 was fuelled using pounds as the unit of measure instead of kilograms, resulting in only half the required amount of fuel being on board. The aircraft used up all available fuel and glided to Gimli Industrial Park Airport where the airliner landed safely. The aircraft is now famously known as the "Gimli Glider."

- A Cessna 208A Caravan, used for skydiving operations at Jenkinsburg, Georgia, crashed following a loss of engine power just after taking off on 29 September 1985. The aircraft had been refuelled with contaminated fuel; all 17 occupants died.

- After a string of mistakes and omissions by the pilots, a Boeing 737-200 operating Varig Flight 254 on 3 September 1989 strayed hundreds of miles off-course, ran out of fuel, and crashed in Brazil's Amazon jungle killing 13 of the occupants. Due to the crew's mistake in flying the aircraft west (270°) instead of north-northeast (027°), the aircraft was not found until four survivors walked onto a farm five days later.
- On 25 January 1990, Avianca Flight 52 was in an extended holding pattern over John F. Kennedy International Airport in New York City due to fog. The Boeing 707-320B was delayed many times before it was given clearance to land. By then, Flight 52 had run out of fuel and crashed into Cove Neck, New York, killing 73.
- A McDonnell Douglas F/A-18A Hornet of the Royal Australian Air Force, serial number A21-41, was lost on 5 June 1991 after the pilot became incapacitated. The aircraft flew until it ran out of fuel and crashed in a remote part of Queensland. The wreckage was not found until over three years later.
- The crew of Indian Airlines Flight 440, an Airbus A300B2-101, executed a missed approach procedure at Hyderabad-Begumpet Airport on 15 November 1993 due to poor visibility. During the missed approach a problem developed when the flaps would not retract fully. After some time trying to solve the flap problem and find somewhere to land near Hyderabad, the crew diverted the aircraft to Madras but because they had to fly slower due to the extended flaps the aircraft ran out of fuel. It landed in a paddy field near Tirupati; there were no fatalities among the 262 occupants but the aircraft was written-off.
- On 23 November 1996, men hijacked Ethiopian Airlines Flight 961 on a short flight segment from Addis Ababa to Nairobi. The hijackers demanded that the aircraft should be flown to Australia despite the pilot telling them that there was insufficient fuel to do so. After three hours of flying along the African coast and across part of the Indian Ocean, the aircraft ran out of fuel and the engines failed. An emergency landing at Grande Comore Island failed when the aircraft landed on the water just off the local beach, killing 125 people including the three hijackers.
- Hapag-Lloyd Flight 3378 on 12 July 2000 had a landing gear problem when it failed to fully retract after takeoff. The pilots decided to continue to Munich but did not realise that their lower speed for much the same hourly fuel consumption (required because the landing gear was not up) meant that they had insufficient fuel to do so. Once the aircraft lost all fuel, the crew attempted an emergency landing at Vienna International Airport but the aircraft landed short of the runway. There were no fatalities.
- On 24 August 2001, Air Transat Flight 236 suffered a fuel leak while crossing the Atlantic Ocean and lost its fuel. The aircraft glided safely to an air base in the Azores.
- TAM Airlines Flight 3084, a Fokker 100, suffered fuel exhaustion on 30 August 2002 because of a leak. The aircraft made an emergency landing in a field with its gear up, killing a cow grazing in the field. No-one on board the aircraft was killed.

- On 13 August 2004, a Convair CV-580 freighter operating as Air Tahoma Flight 185 suffered fuel starvation due to crew mismanagement of the fuel tank system and crashed, killing one of the pilots.
- On 6 August 2005 Tuninter Flight 1153, an ATR 72 en route from Bari, Italy, to Djerba, Tunisia, ditched into the Mediterranean Sea about 18 miles from the city of Palermo. Sixteen of the 39 people on board died. The accident resulted from fuel exhaustion due to the installation of a fuel quantity indicator for an ATR 42 in the ATR 72; the incorrect indicator was over-reading by over 2,000 kg, leading the crew to believe they had enough fuel for the flight.
- On 14 August 2005, fighter jets intercepted Helios Airways Flight 522 after the Helios flight failed to respond to air traffic controllers in Greece. The pilots of the fighter jets reported that they observed no pilots in control of the aircraft, which eventually exhausted its fuel and crashed into a hill near Marathon, Greece, killing all on board. Fuel exhaustion was the final link in the accident chain, but as a consequence of cabin depressurization which had disabled the flight crew.

## Abandoned in-flight aircraft

A number of aircraft have been abandoned by their crew (both intentionally and sometimes accidentally) when the aircraft has continued on its own until fuel exhaustion caused it to crash:

- Some time between midnight and dawn on 5 April 1943, the crew of a Consolidated B-24D Liberator named *Lady Be Good* lost over the Sahara Desert abandoned their aircraft as it was running out of fuel. The aircraft was found in 1959, with the bodies of most of the crew located in 1960. One crew member's body has never been found.
- On 22 October 1987, the pilot of British Aerospace Harrier GR5 serial number *ZD325* was accidentally ejected from his aircraft over Wiltshire, England; the aircraft continued on its own until fuel exhaustion caused it to crash into the Irish Sea. The pilot was killed.
- On 4 July 1989, the pilot of a Soviet Mikoyan-Gurevich MiG-23, presuming he had engine problems, ejected from his aircraft. The aircraft continued on its own, flying out of the former East Germany into the West German Air Defence Zone and was then escorted by United States Air Force F-15s until it ran out of fuel and crashed into a house in Belgium, killing the occupant of the house.

## See also

- Vapour lock
- Engine knocking
- List of accidents and incidents involving airliners by airline
- Air safety
- Flight planning
- Flight plan
- Step climb
- Flight dispatcher

- Aviator
- Flight engineer

# References

## Bibliography

- Wilson, Stewart. *Phantom, Hornet and Skyhawk in Australian Service*. Weston Creek ACT, Australia: Aerospace Publications Pty. Ltd., 1993. ISBN 1-875671-03-X.

## External links

- Fuel Starvation in General Aviation [1]

# Engine cart

## Engine cart

An **engine cart** is an engine support on rollers used at an engine test stand. For example, the combustion engine is mounted on this mobile support for holding the engine in an accurate position during the test.

Compared to a fixed support, the engine cart is used for preparing the combustion engine outside the test stand in a separate rigging area. The transport from the rigging area to the test room is made manual.

### External Link: Companies

- ACS [1]
- HORIBA Automotive Test Systems [2]
- Superflow [3]

# VAG-COM

## VAG-COM

| | |
|---|---|
| **Original author(s)** | Uwe M. Ross |
| **Developer(s)** | Ross-Tech, LLC |
| **Initial release** | May 16, 2000 |
| **Stable release** | 10.6 / June 30, 2010 |
| **Development status** | Active |
| **Operating system** | Microsoft Windows |
| **Platform** | Microsoft Windows |
| **Size** | ~13.5 MB (for self-installing EXE file) |
| **Available in** | English, Czech, Danish, Dutch, French, German, Greek, Hungarian, Italian, Polish, Portuguese, Romanian, Spanish, Swedish, Turkish |
| **Type** | Automotive OBD |
| **License** | Proprietary |
| **Website** | Ross-Tech.com [1] |

**VAG-COM**, now officially known as **VCDS** (an acronym for "VAG-COM Diagnostic System"), is a third party Microsoft Windows-based software package, developed and produced by Ross-Tech, LLC since May 2000. It is primarily used for diagnostics and adjustments of Volkswagen Group motor vehicles, including Volkswagen Passenger Cars, Audi, SEAT, and Škoda automobiles, along with Volkswagen Commercial Vehicles.

VCDS will perform most of the functions of the expensive electronic diagnostic tools available only to official dealers, like the current *VAS 505x* series diagnostic tools. In the past, these dealership-only tools have prevented owners, and many small independent repair shops from performing some fundamental tasks, such as diagnosing problems, diesel ignition timing, modification of convenience options such as automatic door unlocking, coding a replacement electronic control unit (ECU) or key to the vehicle, and monitoring of many vehicle sensors for diagnosing problems. Unlike generic on-board diagnostics (OBD-II / EOBD), VCDS uses the more in-depth Volkswagen Group-specific manufacturer protocol commands, which allows the user to access all diagnostic capable vehicle systems — even in vehicles which are not covered by generic OBD-II/EOBD (e.g. pre-1996). In general, there are two ways to use this software, either as a package (software *and* hardware) distributed by the manufacturer or their agents, or, by building own interface hardware and using it with the public-available but limited shareware version of the software.

VCDS is also capable of interfacing vehicles which use the generic OBD-II/EOBD protocols. However, the OBD-II and EOBD standards only allow for limited diagnostics, and no adjustments to any of the ECUs.

# External links

- Ross-Tech.com [1] - official site
- OpenDiag Schematics & PCB Layout [2] - a DIY OBD-II serial adapter that can be used with VAG-COM
- Ross-Tech wiki page [3] - experimental, but has a large database of VAG-specific fault codes, and some diagnostics procedures
- en.OpenOBD.org - self diagnostics [4] - a site with detailed examples of 'long coding' settings
  - de.OpenOBD.org [5] - (German) section of the above, with more in-depth settings available
- A useful list of coding/measurement procedures (using VAG-COM) [6]

# Breakdown (vehicle)

## Breakdown (vehicle)

A vehicle **breakdown** is the operational failure of a motor vehicle in such a way that the underlying problem prevents the vehicle from being operated at all, or impedes the vehicle's operation so much, that it is very difficult or nearly impossible, or dangerous to operate, or else at risk of causing further damage to the vehicle. Vehicle breakdowns can occur for a large number of reasons. Depending on the nature of the problem, the vehicle may or may not need to be towed to an automobile repair shop.

An overheated Vauxhall Carlton stopped on Tottenham Court Road, London

## Levels of breakdown

There are various levels of a vehicle's disability.

### Total breakdown

A *total breakdown* is when the vehicle becomes totally immobile and cannot be driven even a short distance to reach a repair shop, thereby necessitating a tow. This can occur for a variety of reasons, including complete engine failure, which is commonly caused by not regularly getting the vehicle thoroughly inspected and maintained/repaired by a licensed mechanic. A breakdown can also occur from a dead starter motor or battery, although a dead battery may be able to be temporarily resolved with a jump start.

When a total breakdown occurs, the motorist may be able to have the service paid for by a roadside assistance plan. This may be available through an organization like the AAA, the vehicle's manufacturer, the vehicle insurance policy, or in some cases, another service the driver subscribes to, such as a mobile phone carrier.

## Partial breakdown

In a *partial breakdown*, the vehicle may still be operable, but its operation may become more limited or more dangerous, or else its continued operation may contribute to further damage to the vehicle. Often, when this occurs, it may be possible to drive the vehicle to a garage, thereby avoiding a tow.

Some common causes of a partial breakdown include overheating, brake failure, or frequent stalling.

With other problems, the driver may be able to operate the vehicle seemingly normally for some time, but the vehicle will need an eventual repair. These include grinding brakes, rough idle (often caused by the need for a tune-up), or poor shock absorption. Many vehicle owners with personal economic difficulty or a busy schedule may wait longer than they should to get necessary repairs made to their vehicles, thereby increasing damage or else causing more danger.

## See also

- Vehicle recovery
- Battery
- Car insurance
- Car warranty
- Crash and vehicle breakdown scenes
- Emergency road service
- Mechanical restoration
- Tow truck

## External links

- Non-profit National Institute for Automotive Service Excellence (ASE) [1].
- Massive archive of repair questions and answers. [2].

# Auto maintenance

## Auto maintenance

**Auto maintenance** describes the act of inspecting or testing the condition of car subsystems (e.g., engine) and servicing or replacing parts and fluids. Regular maintenance is critical to ensure the safety, reliability, drivability, comfort and longevity of a car. During preventive maintenance, a number of parts are replaced to avoid major damage or for safety reasons, e.g. timing belt replacement.

Oil being drained from a GMC Sport Utility Vehicle.

The actual schedule of car maintenance varies depending on the year, make, and model of a car, its driving conditions and driver behavior. Car makers recommend the so-called extreme or the ideal service schedule based on impact parameters such as

- number of trips and distance traveled per trip per day
- extreme hot or cold climate conditions
- mountainous, dusty or de-iced roads
- heavy stop-and-go vs. long-distance cruising
- towing a trailer or other heavy load

Experienced service advisors in dealerships and independent shops recommend schedule intervals, which are often in between the ideal or extreme service schedule. They base it on the driving conditions and behavior of the car owner or driver.

Common car maintenance tasks include:

- Car wash
- check/replace the engine oil and replace oil filters
- check/replace fuel filters
- inspect or replace windshield wipers
- check or refill windshield washer fluid
- inspect tires for pressure and wear
- Tire balancing
- Tire rotation
- Wheel alignment

- check, clean or replace battery terminals and top up battery fluid
- inspect or replace brake pads
- check or flush brake fluid
- check or flush transmission fluid
- check or flush power steering fluid
- check and flush engine coolant
- inspect or replace spark plugs
- inspect or replace air filter
- inspect or replace timing belt and other belts
- lubricate locks, latches, hinges
- check all lights
- tighten chassis nuts and bolts
- check if rubber boots are cracked and need replacement
- test electronics, e.g., Anti-lock braking system or ABS
- read fault codes from the Engine control unit

Some tasks that have equivalent service intervals are combined into one single service known as a tune-up. In modern cars, where electronics control most of the car's functions, the traditional tune-up doesn't apply anymore. Maintenance jobs like a tune-up used to mean getting the engine's performance back on track. Today embedded software takes care of it by constantly checking thousands of sensor signals, compensating for worn-out spark plugs, clogged filters, etc. The so-called limp-home function allows driving on limited power when the engine is in trouble. In the old days this might have meant a breakdown.

Routine car maintenance is related to vehicle fuel economy. Some of the procedures include:

- Ensure tires are properly inflated. The owners manual for the vehicle will indicate the proper pressure to inflate you tires to. Decreased tire pressure increases the rolling resistance of your tires and decreases fuel economy, and may also increase tire wear and impair performance.
- The thermostat, oxygen or O2 sensor should be replaced either at a manufacturer recommended interval or when a electronic fault code/ low temperature problem is detected. Electronically fuel injected vehicles have an O2 sensor or sensors in their exhaust system which helps the vehicles computer determine how to optimize fuel economy. These O2 sensors may need to be changed periodically for a vehicle to optimize it's air fuel mixture and maximize it's fuel economy.
- Insure vehicle air filters are clean. Black or otherwise dirty air filters make your engine work harder to get enough air for proper combustion and decrease its efficiency; however, electronically fuel injected cars can automatically compensate for the decreased air flow caused by a dirty air filter and experience relatively little decrease in fuel economy. Most owners' manuals will recommend a service interval at which to change the air filter, but periodic visual inspection is the best way to ensure that the air filter is clean.

- Using the recommended weight of oil can decrease the burden on the engine. Heavier oil weights, such as 20W-50, are harder to maneuver through the engine than, for example, 10W-30 or 5W-20 oils. The result can cause a decrease in fuel economy.

In some countries, the completed services are recorded in a service book which is rubber-stamped by the service center upon completion of each service. A complete service history usually adds to the resale value of a vehicle.

## See also

- Auto mechanic
- Automobile repair shop
- Mechanical engineering

# Plastic headlight restoration

## Plastic headlight restoration

**Plastic headlight restoration** is the act of refinishing aged headlights that have succumbed to **headlamp oxidation** and other environmental hazards of travel, weather, and exposure to caustic chemicals. This condition which results in cloudy lenses is known for causing reduced night time visibility for travellers as the condition becomes worse.

Most often the solution is to resurface the lens by lightly sanding the affected surface with different grades or grits of finishing paper until the oxidation is removed and then applying a protective finishing coat to re-seal the surface of the restored headlight.

Recent years have seen a dramatic increase in the number of manufacturers offering such products to combat this prevalent problem. Although seemingly expensive at generally $20 to $50 USD per product, do-it-yourself headlight restoration in the long run can effectively save consumers hundreds of dollars over replacement of damaged plastic headlight covers. A cheaper alternative is plain white toothpaste. It works just as well albeit it takes more elbow grease.

Plastic headlight restoration is growing exponentially because auto manufacturers continue to make vehicles with plastic headlight lenses that, without proper care and maintenance, result in cloudy foggy headlights. After as little as two or three years on the road, they become so "cloudy" that they actually output less light than is needed to legally do their job. The problem affects virtually every make of car and truck, foreign or domestic.

# Chilton Company

## Chilton Company

**Chilton Company** (AKA Chilton Printing Co., Chilton Publishing Co., Chilton Book Co. and Chilton Research Services) is a former publishing company, most famous for its trade magazines, and automotive manuals. It also provided conference and market research services to a wide variety of industries.

In its 93 years, Chilton grew from a small single magazine publisher to a leading publisher of business to business magazines, consumer and professional automotive manuals, craft and hobby books and a large well known marketing research company. In its early years, its flagship magazine was *Iron Age* - in 1955, Chilton's profit reached $1 million for the first time, of which *Iron Age* accounted for $750,000. By 1980, *Iron Age*'s revenue and status had declined due to the reduction in the size of the US metalworking manufacturing industry, and *Jewelers Circular Keystone* captured the position of most profitable magazine.

While Chilton had leading magazines in several different industries, the Chilton name was most strongly associated with the consumer and professional automotive manuals. That is why the Chilton brand of do-it-yourself automotive manuals still exists ten years after the Chilton Company has ceased operations.

### History

The company traces its origins back to July 1896 and the first issue of *Cycle Trade Journal*, which was edited by James Artman, the first president of the future Chilton Company. In 1899 the magazine's name changed to *Cycle & Automobile Trade Journal*. A 1900 magazine masthead listed Musselman & Buzby as the exclusive advertising representatives for Cycle & Automobile Trade Journal. In 1900 George Buzby, C. A. Musselman and James Artman merged their companies to form the *Trade Advertising & Publishing Co*. The new company expanded its product offerings to include automotive catalogs, booklets, circulars and posters.

The name Chilton was selected from a list of the passenger names on the Mayflower. The earliest use of the corporate name *Chilton Company* was in 1904, as shown on a corporate seal which reads "Chilton Company of Pennsylvania, incorporated March 31, 1904". In 1907 the three partners purchased a printing company, which they named the *Chilton Printing Company*, only publicly adopting the name *Chilton Company* in 1910.

In March 1911 Chilton published the first issue of *Commercial Car Journal*. In February 1912, the original *Cycle & Automobile Trade Journal* was renamed *Automobile Trade Journal*; the magazine was eventually merged into Motor Age magazine.

In 1923 Chilton was sold to United Publishers Corp of New York for $1,635,000, and Artman and Buzby retired. In the same year, Chilton opened their new printing plant located at 56th and Chestnut Streets in Philadelphia. This location was to serve as the Chilton Company corporate headquarters starting in the late 1940's.

Shortly after the purchase United Publishers merged their Class Journal subsidiary and Chilton into what became known as the *Chilton Class Journal Co*, with C. A. Musselman as its president. This merger brought several future flag ship magazines (such as Iron Age, Motor Age, Dry Goods Economist, Jewelers Circular, Hardware Age and Automotive Industries) into the Chilton stable of magazines.

In 1934 a complete reorganization of the company took place. J. Howard Pew provided an infusion of cash and saved the company from bankruptcy, in exchange for a majority of the stock. All subsidiaries were merged into one company and incorporated in the state of Delaware as *Chilton Company*. While the cash infusion from J. Howard Pew saved the company, it also proved to be the single biggest inhibitor to its growth, as Pew did not permit Chilton to seek outside funding for acquisitions. As a result, Chilton Company's growth over the next thirty years lagged behind other competitors such as McGraw Hill and Penton.

George Buzby's son G. C. (Carroll) Buzby became president of Chilton in the early 1950s and remained the Chief Executive Officer until his retirement in the late 1960's. George C. Buzby died of cancer in 1970.

In 1979, Chilton Company was purchased by the American Broadcasting Company, and became an operating unit of ABC Publishing. In 1985 Capital Cities purchased ABC and in 1996 the Walt Disney Company purchased Capital Cities/ABC. Over-extended financially by its acquisition of Capital Cities ABC, Disney needed to sell assets in order to reduce its debt, and Chilton, despite its status and recognition as an excellent business to business magazine publisher, was not considered a core business. Disney therefore decided to split up and sell the Chilton Company profit centers to multiple buyers:

* Reed Elsevier purchased the Chilton building and the magazine division for $444 million in 1997.
* The Hearst Corporation purchased the assets of the Chilton Professional Automotive group.
* Nichols Publishing purchased the *Chilton Consumer Automotive* group. In 2003 Nichols sold the do-it-yourself automotive print manuals to Haynes Publishing Group (publishers of Haynes Manuals), and the remaining automotive assets to Thompson Learning; in 2007 Thomson Learning became Cengage Learning.

## Offices

After the acquisition by United Publishers in 1923, the corporate office moved to New York City. In 1955 all the former United Publishers magazines and their staffs relocated from New York City to the corporate headquarters at 56th and Chestnut Streets in Philadelphia. In 1968 Chilton moved their corporate offices to Decker Square in Bala Cynwyd, Pennsylvania. This served as temporary headquarters until 1972 when Chilton moved into its new corporate headquarters building in Radnor, Pennsylvania.

## Fiction publishing

After many years of publishing business to business magazines and automotive manuals, Chilton published the celebrated science fiction novels *Dune* by Frank Herbert (1965) and *The Witches of Karres* (1966) by James H. Schmitz. Each was nominated for a Hugo Award for Best Novel in its respective year, and *Dune* won the award. *Dune* became the first of a series of six novels by Frank Herbert, which were followed by many books, mostly prequels, by his son, Brian Herbert, and Kevin J. Anderson, an unrelated but experienced author. Of these books, Chilton only published the first. In this respect, Chilton resembled the Naval Institute Press. The Naval Institute Press normally publishes naval history books and other textbooks used at the United States Naval Academy but in 1984 it published Tom Clancy's first novel—a surprise best seller—then allowed other publishers to handle Clancy's later books and returned to obscurity.

## See also

- Clymer repair manual
- Cyclepedia Repair Manuals
- Haynes Manuals

## External links

- About Chilton [1] - from the website of Cengage, current publisher of Chilton's automotive manuals.

# Car ramp

## Car ramp

A **car ramp** provides a simple method of raising a vehicle from the ground in order to access the underside of the vehicle.

# Remote diagnostics

## Remote diagnostics

Remote Diagnostics refers to ability to diagnose a given symptom, issue or problem from a distance. Instead of the subject being colocated with the person or system doing the diagnostics, with remote diagnostics, the subjects can be separated by physical distant (E.g., earth-moon). Information exchange occurs either by wire or wireless.

When limiting to systems, a general accepted definition is: 'To Improve reliability of vital or capital-intensive installations and reduce the maintenance costs by avoiding unplanned maintenance, by monitoring the condition of the system remotely. '

Process elements for remote diagnostics:

- Remotely monitor selected vital system parameters
- Analysis of data to detect trends
- Comparison with known or expected behavior data
- After detected performance degradation, predict the failure moment by extrapolation
- Order parts and/or plan maintenance, to be executed when really necessary, but in time to prevent a failure or stop

Typical uses:

- medical use (see Remote guidance)
- Formula One racecars
- space (Apollo project and others)
- Telephone systems like a PABX
- aeroplanes

The reasons for RD can be one of more of these aspects:

- limit local personnel to a minimum (Gemini, Apollo capsules: too tight to fit all technicians)
- limit workload of local personnel
- limit risks (exposure to dangerous environments)
- central expertise (locally solve small problems, remotely/centralized solve complex problems by experts)
- efficiency: reduce travel time to get expert & system or subject together

# A Web Broker Architecture for Remote Machine Diagnostics

Machine remote diagnosis allows initiation of the best course of action for problem resolution. When tracking problems or strange behaviour on a PLC controlled machine, it is often difficult or even impossible to correct the problem if it cannot be reproduced by the service staff. In the worst case scenario, the machine needs to be serviced on site to identify the problem, involving a local technician with all the communication, language and accent problems that may arise with the machine builder.

A simple and cost-effective way to remotely maintain and service industrial machinery worldwide consists of using a Web broker architecture. As the Internet grew, it provided an opportunity for free or public long distance communication for remote access. Now combined with cellular technologies that provide wireless communication or DSL based technologies, this offers the market new communication media for accessing devices. However, DSL based technologies require installing a dedicated line to the machine location, while cellular technologies requires that wireless receivers are available in the vicinity of the machine providing adequate coverage for good communication.

# Remote Diagnostic & Maintenance

Remote Diagnostic & Maintenance refers to both diagnoses of the fault or faults and taking corrective (maintenance) actions, like changing settings to improve performance or prevent problems like breakdown, wear & tear. RDM can replace manpower at location by experts on a central location, in order to save manpower or prevent hazardous situations (space for instance).

# External links

- Onstar Diagnostics [1]
- eWON Industrial Routers [2]
- Talk2M, Internet Remote Access for Machines [3]

# The Garage (TV)

## The Garage (TV)

| The Garage | |
|---|---|
| **Format** | Documentary film/Reality television |
| **Starring** | Graham "Jock" Campbell<br>Alicia Campbell<br>Glyn Bennett<br>Sandy Fairbairn<br>Ed Blasi<br>Lindsey Baldwin<br>Danielle Christie<br>Claire Watts<br>Ricky Coates<br>Gemma Pugsley<br>Rob Rowles |
| **Country of origin** | ▦ United Kingdom |
| **No. of seasons** | 3 |
| **Production** | |
| **Location(s)** | Marbella, Spain |
| **Running time** | 50 minutes (Discovery Channel) (without commercials) |
| **Broadcast** | |
| **Original channel** | Discovery Channel<br>Discovery HD |
| **Picture format** | 480i (SDTV) |
| **Original run** | 2005 – 2007 |
| **External links** | |
| Official website [1] | |

**The Garage** is a television programme following the staff of English Mobile Mechanics in Marbella Spain. The programme follows the activities of the garage and initially it followed new staff hires as they adjusted to life in Spain whilst coping with their new jobs and their boss, Jock Campbell. Four out of the five new recruits eventually announced that they were leaving and vacated their positions.

# Episode list

## Series one

Series one is a seven-part show without episode titles.

## Series two

S02E01, Jock's Back!

S02E02, Airbags All Round

S02E03, Ed The Hero

S02E04, Ed's Clutch Déjà vu

S02E05, Sandy's Story

S02E06, A Hard Week's Delegation

S02E07, Jock the 2nd–hand Car Dealer

S02E08, Love is in the Air

S02E09, Living for the Weekend

S02E10, Against the Clock

S02E11, The End of the Summer

S02E12, Final Best Bits

## Series 3

S03E01, New Blood

S03E02, Ferrari

S03E03, Subtle Engineering

S03E04, Spanner in the Works

S03E05, Old Jag

S03E06, No More Girls

S03E07, Hot and Bothered

S03E08, Locking Horns

S03E09, Lost and Losing It

S03E10, Leaks

S03E11, Dream Cars

S03E12, The Garage Refueled

S03E13, Adventures

## External links

- English Mobile Mechanics [2]
- Discovery Channel's pages on the show [1]
- Sandy Fairbairn's own garage/website [3]
- Danielle Christie's Website [4]

# Paintless dent repair

## Paintless dent repair

**Paintless dent repair** (PDR), also known as "paintless dent removal", is a collection of techniques for removing minor dents and dings from the body of a motor vehicle. A wide range of damage can be repaired using PDR; however, usually if there is paint damage, PDR may be unsuitable.

The most common practical use for PDR is the repair of hail damage, door dings, minor body creases, and minor bumper indentations. The techniques can also be applied to help prepare the damaged panel for paint. Such applications are referred to as "push to paint", or "push for paint".

Limiting factors for a successful repair using PDR include the flexibility of the paint, and the amount the metal has been stretched by the damage incurred. Hence, often extremely sharp dents and creases may not be repairable - at least not without painting afterwards.

### Methods of Repair

The most common methods of paintless dent repair utilize metal rods and body picks to push the dents out from the inner side of the body panel being repaired. Also, glue may be used from the outside of the panel to pull the dents out. In either case, fine-tuning of the repair often involves "tapping" down the repair to remove small high spots, making the surface flat. Paintless Dent Repair may be used on both aluminum and steel panels. If a technician pushes too hard when creating these high spots, the paint will split and the repair is ruined. Quality technicians can use these high spots that are barely visible to match the texture of the paint.

The technology of PDR has been around for many years. Fluorescent lighting, or in some cases a light-reflection board, is used to see the shadows created by the deformation of the dent. This is an important aspect of the repair process. Without a Paintless Dent Repair light board or reflector board, the fine detail of the process is unseen, and the technician cannot locate their tool specifically and cannot remove the damage accurately. The process of Paintless Dent Repair requires a technician to specifically push exact locations of metal to a precise height, which can only be witnessed with use of a PDR reading instrument, such as a Paintless Dent Repair reflector board or Paintless Dent Repair light.

Paintless dent removal takes time to learn it is more of an art than a specific set of skills. The ability to successfully remove dents and dings is learned through trial and error. An untrained individual can actually damage a dent if attempting a repair without the correct skills and knowledge. Paintless dent removal technicians can be located throughout the country by searching for their services online.

# Service (motor vehicle)

## Service (motor vehicle)

A **motor vehicle service** is a series of maintenance procedures carried out at a set time interval or after the vehicle has travelled a certain distance. The service intervals are specified by the vehicle manufacturer in a service schedule and some modern cars display the due date for the next service electronically on the instrument panel.

Maintenance tasks commonly carried out during a motor vehicle service include:

Mechanics at a **Car Service Center**.

- Change the engine oil
- Replace the oil filter
- Replace the air filter
- Replace the fuel filter
- Replace the spark plugs
- Tune the engine
- Check level and refill brake fluid
- Check level and refill power steering fluid
- Check level and refill Automatic Transmission Fluid
- Grease and lubricate components
- Inspect and replace the timing belt if needed
- Check condition of the tyres

Mechanical parts that may cause the car to cease transmission or prove unsafe for the road are also noted and advised upon.

In the United Kingdom, few parts that are not inspected on the MOT test are inspected and advised upon a Service Inspection.

These include:

- Clutch
- Gearbox
- Car Battery

- Engine components (further inspections than MOT)

Mechanical parts of the vehicle which deteriorated below pass standard since testing are inspected and advised accordingly.

# Eastwood Company

## Eastwood Company

| Type | Automotive Parts and Supplies Retailer |
|------|----------------------------------------|
| Founder(s) | Curt Strohacker |
| Owner(s) | Curt Strohacker |

**The Eastwood Company** is a Pottstown, Pennsylvania, USA, company, specialising in automotive restoration and repair tools and supplies. Founded in 1978 by Curt Strohacker, Eastwood sold products such as rust prevention coatings and power coating supplies by mail order, through car show, and on the internet.

## Corporate History

In August 1978, Curt Strohacker founded the Eastwood Company with the intent to deliver professional-quality tools to automotive hobbyists. During high school, Curt had worked in a service station, but he also repaired cars in his free time and he realized that he could put this technical knowledge to use in the retail sector. The first Eastwood catalog consisted of eight black and white pages of metal-finishing equipment, but by the early 1980s annual circulation had reached 5,000 and continued operation required the services of a professional list house. In addition to catalog marketing, Eastwood also sold directly to restorers at select car shows.

In August 1983, both the Mercedes-Benz and BMW car clubs unexpectedly endorsed an Eastwood car wash brush – sales multiplied and the staff soon doubled. The development of the Eastwood Spot-Weld Gun, a tool which duplicates the industrial spot-welds found on virtually every metal-bodied car, proved even more fortunate for the growing retailer. At that time, most of Eastwood's new business came from magazine ads in about a dozen publications. By the end of 1985, company advertisements appeared in over fifty magazines, including Hot Rod Magazine, Car Craft, and Popular Mechanics. Accordingly, the catalog matured as well - in 1986, over 100,000 auto restorers received a 96-page, four-color cover Eastwood catalog; by the end of the decade, annual circulation surpassed 500,000.

In 1997, Eastwood introduced the HotCoat Powder Coating System. Though powder coating produces a more durable and attractive finish, the high cost and requisite skill had long confined its use to professional shops, a stranglehold which Eastwood intended to break. In September of the following year, Eastwood received the Pennsylvania Governor's Award for "Environmental Excellence", recognizing the low environmental impact of the HotCoat system. In 1999, the Automotive Restoration Market Organization (ARMO) awarded HotCoat the "Best New Product" for that year.

In 2003, Eastwood introduced its Interchangeable English Wheel and Planishing Hammer, enabling a wider audience to access high-end metal shaping tools. By emphasizing economy in manufacturing and the use of a universal frame, Eastwood was able to offer these products at less than $1000. The ARMO recognized this achievement with a "People's Choice" award in 2004.

In order to keep pace with the explosion of e-commerce, Eastwood launched websites for its tool catalog (www.eastwood.com) and HotCoat (www.hotcoat.com). The sites contain information about new products and promotions, in addition to providing potential new customers with the opportunity to request an Eastwood catalog. Furthermore, Eastwood's site contains technical articles related to popular products, a blog and forum, and a video library. Beginning in January 1999, the sites also allowed customers to order the full product line, integrating purchasing systems from a secure site.

Though online retail has become increasingly prominent, Eastwood continues to publish a monthly, full-size catalog. In November 1999, the company broke ground for a new facility north of Philadelphia, in Pottstown, Pennsylvania. Following an eight month construction project, Eastwood completely relocated to Pottstown in July of the following year.

## External links

- The Eastwood Company [1]
- Eastwood on Facebook [2]
- Eastwood YouTube [3]
- Eastwood MySpace [4]

# Service Labor Time Standards

## Service Labor Time Standards

*"SLTS" redirects here. For the Nirvana song commonly abbreviated to "SLTS," see Smells Like Teen Spirit.*

**Service Labor Time Standards** or **SLTSs** are used by automotive manufacturers to determine the time required to repair a particular malfunctioning part on one of their automobiles.

The SLTS is the benchmark for other aftermarket repair facilities to determine how much to charge customers when they have their vehicle repaired. These times were all determined by actual (alleged) disassembly and reassembly of the affected part(s). Using several workers disassembly and reassembly times were taken and an average was established. Times for retrieving the automobile, diagnosing the concern, retrieving the part(s) from the parts department, and a test drive if necessary was included to fully establish the SLTS. An experienced automotive technician could potentially repair a vehicle faster than a technician that has minimal experience and must consult with the manual to properly diagnose and repair the same concern.

# Tune-up

# Tune-up

A **tune-up** (also known as a **major service**) is regular maintenance performed on an automobile, or more generally, any internal combustion engine. Most automobile manufacturers recommend a tune-up be performed at an interval of 30,000 miles (48,000 km) or two years, whichever comes first.

## Justification

As with all preventive maintenance performed on an automobile, tune-ups can prevent myriad problems from occurring on a vehicle. The filters replaced can clog with use and prevent flow, starving the engine of fuel or air. Spark plugs have a recommended service lifetime of either 30,000 miles or, in the case of platinum or iridium plugs, 60,000 to 100,000 miles (96,000 to 160,000 km), and old spark plugs may cause engine misfire.

## See also

* Engine tuning

# Number matching

## Number matching

**Number matching** or **matching numbers** is a term often used in the collector car industry to describe cars with original major components, or major components that match one another.

Many times these major components contain dates, casting numbers, model numbers, Vehicle Identification Numbers (VIN), stamped numbers, or codes that can match the original components that were on the car when it was new.

### Definition

The term "number matching" (or "matching numbers") is a term used in the collector car industry to describe the authenticity of collectible or investment quality cars. Number matching generally means that a particular car still contains its original major components or has major components that match exactly the major components the car had when it was new. These "major components" are not always agreed on. The appearance of a number matching car likely could not distinguished from an original car. A site by the name numbermatching.com (direct link removed since Firefox reports this site as "suspicious." Visit at own risk) has established a standard of specifications for a common definition of "number matching" and can certify them according to their company's definition.

### Major Components

The car's major not maching components are parts such as the engine, transmission, rear-axle assembly, and frame of the car. Many times these components contain dates, casting numbers, model numbers, VIN, stamped numbers, or codes that can match the original components that were on the car when it was new. In some cases intake manifolds, exhaust manifolds, body panels, and carburettors could also be considered major components.

### Minor Components

Minor components are components that would not dramatically affect the overall value of a car, regardless of being original or not. These are parts that are commonly replaced due to regular wear and tear. Parts such as the interior fabric, paint, chrome trim, brakes, instruments, electrical components and wiring are considered minor components.

# How does number matching work?

The numbers or casting dates on the major components of a car must be present and fall in a particular order. For example, an engine's assembly date must come before the build date of the car, and the casting dates must come before the assembly date of the engine because an engine assembly date (the date the engine was assembled, usually at a different location) could not be after the assembly date of the whole car. Engines are assembled prior to being installed in the car at the factory. Therefore, the assembly date of the car would have to be after the assembly date of the engine. Casting dates (the dates formed in the metal of a component at the foundry) could not be after the assembly date of the engine. And casting dates would need to be well in advance of the assembly date of the engine. Numbers and dates help track an accurate history of how a car was built and when and where the car and the parts used to create the car were made.

If a car has number matching major components it helps define how collectible a car is. Number matching cars typically will have a much greater value than non-number matching cars.

# Why are number matching cars collectible?

Number matching cars are collectible because they are much rarer than non-number matching cars. Number matching cars represent a look back in history at what was occurring in the automobile industry, and it may be for this reason that matching numbers are tied to collector car values.

# Technical Service Bulletin

## Technical Service Bulletin

**Technical Service Bulletins**, or TSBs, are recommended procedures for repairing vehicles. Not to be confused with recalls, a TSB is issued by a vehicle manufacturer when there are several occurrences of an unanticipated problem. TSBs can range from vehicle-specific to covering entire product lines and break down the specified repair into a step-by-step process. While sometimes written by engineers employed by OEM's, the majority are authored by the first automotive technician to come up with a repair procedure. Because certain problems may have more than one cause or there are sometimes more than one way to fix a problem, it's somewhat common for there to be more than one TSB for the same problem.

One major difference between a recall and a TSB in the automotive industry is that a recall usually evolves out of safety issues at the behest of an organization like the National Highway Traffic Safety Administration (NHTSA). The ensuing recall maintenance/repair work is usually done at no charge to the car owner, regardless of the car's warranty status. Dealers are usually under no mandate to call in cars for which there are TSBs to do the related repairs. Nor is there an obligation to do the TSB repairs for free or at reduced charges to the owner.

Some benefits of an automotive TSB are that by widely circulating among dealership service departments and mechanics an engineering-level description and solution for a problem common to type, year, make or model of car, a well-managed TSB process can save technicians troubleshooting time, provide and organized, itemized repair procedures, and standardize the repair process. This can also enhance the quality of the maintenance since it tends to be supported by repair history and high-level diagnostic procedure decisions.

NPR's "Car Talk" show duo, Tom Magliozzi and brother Ray Magliozzi (also known as "Click and Clack"), describe TSBs, saying, "They really just contain advice from the company to the mechanics who fix their cars," in this S.F. Chronicle article, "Technical Service Bulletins Explained." [1] But this Edmunds article, "How Can a Technical Service Bulletin Help Me?" [2] states that if there's a TSB for your particular problem, and it's verifiable by the dealer, then the repair is free to cars within the warranty period.

# Italian tuneup

## Italian tuneup

An **Italian tuneup** usually refers to a process whereby the operator of a motor vehicle runs the engine at full load for extended periods in order to burn carbon buildup from the combustion chambers and exhaust system. It is performed after a traditional tuneup and often accompanied by an addition of fuel system cleaner to the fuel tank. It is particularly useful for vehicles that are only operated at low speeds on short journeys, and for diesel vehicles prior to emissions testing.

### History

The origin of the Italian tuneup comes from Ferrari. Owners would use these performance cars as daily drivers and never run them hard which causes the engine to build up enough carbon inside to affect performance. Mechanics would perform a "tuneup" by driving several laps around a race track to get the engine hot enough to burn out the built up carbon. Cars before the advent of modern engine lubricants and fuels, often had a 'de-coke' by hand, after removing the cylinder head, as a scheduled service operation.

# Deglazing (engine mechanics)

## Deglazing (engine mechanics)

**Deglazing** is a process by which the surface of an engine cylinder is roughened to create friction between the moving parts and allow engine oil to grip the sides of the cylinder.

### Details

In a gasoline or diesel engine, the pistons ride up and down within the engine maintaining a tight seal via the piston rings. Over time, the constant rubbing of the rings against the cylinder wall can polish it to a very smooth finish. This creates problems in two ways. First, the lubricating oil in the engine will not adhere properly to the mirror smooth surface, and friction is increased. Secondly, while breaking in newly installed piston rings, a minute amount of wear must occur between rings and cylinder wall in order to seat the rings properly, and ensure a gas-tight seal. If the cylinder walls are too smooth, this wear will not occur, with the rings "skating" over the polished surface.

In order to correct the situation, a mechanic can take the engine apart, and *deglaze* the cylinders, usually using an abrasive. This creates a roughly 45 degree angle crosshatching of tiny grooves in the cylinder wall, and restores the engines performance.

# Engine crane

## Engine crane

## Engine crane

An **engine crane** is a common repair tool used in vehicle repair shops to remove or install gasoline or diesel engines in small and crowded vehicle engine compartments. It uses a heavy cantilevered support structure to hold the engine in mid-air so that the mechanic can carefully connect or disconnect fragile hoses and wires on the engine to the frame of the vehicle.

Engine cranes are typically mounted on large casters so than an engine can be lifted straight up out of an engine compartment and then rolled away from the immobile vehicle frame.

The engine crane is commonly used in combination with the engine stand so that the removed engine can be rotated in midair to provide access to underside surfaces of the engine.

# Turtle Wax

# Turtle Wax

| Type | Privately Held |
|---|---|
| Founded | 1941 (as Plastone) |
| Headquarters | Willowbrook, Illinois |
| Key people | Denis J. Healy (Chief Executive Officer and President) Tom Healy (Vice President of Global Sales & Marketing) |
| Employees | 51-200 |
| Website | TurtleWax.com [1] |

**Turtle Wax** is a manufacturer of automotive appearance products. The company was founded by Benjamin Hirsch in 1941 and is currently headquartered in Willowbrook, Illinois. Turtle Wax is the largest automotive appearance products company in the world and distributes its products in more than 90 countries.

The company's primary product lines include cleaning and polishing products for cars including glass, painted surfaces, uncoated metals, leather, wheels, and tires, for both the retail consumer and professional detailer markets. Turtle Wax also offers automotive performance chemicals such as engine treatment products and formula oils.

Additionally, the company operates full-service car wash facilities in the Chicago Metropolitan area and the Kansas City Metropolitan Area.

## External links

- Distributors of Turtle Wax in the UK [2]
- Turtle Wax homepage [1]
- Turtle Wax European homepage [3]

# Rain-X

# Rain-X

**Rain-X** is a line of consumer automotive and surface care products produced by SOPUS Products (formerly Quaker State), a subsidiary of Royal Dutch Shell. Industrial Rain-X products are produced by Ecolab and used in carwashes and other industrial applications. The most well known Rain-X product is a synthetic hydrophobic surface-applied product that causes water to bead, most commonly used on glass automobile surfaces. Rain-X was originally registered as a trademark in 1972 by Unelko and sold to Quaker State in 1997. Rain-X branded products are distributed by Shell Car Care International Limited in the U.K.

## Products

The Rain-X brand includes seven categories of products: wiper blades, glass and windshield treatments, plastic cleaners, windshield washer fluid, car washes, car wax, and bug and tar washes.

Competing products include PGW's (formerly of PPG) Aquapel. Rain-X's brand awareness in the automotive consumer product segment is particularly high, being claimed as second only to Windex.

## Uses

Due to its general water repellent properties, the original Rain-X formulation is used in a wide variety of consumer, commercial and industrial settings. The primary use of Rain-X is for automotive applications. Commercially sold "Original Glass Treatment" is the original and most well known Rain-X branded product. It is a hydrophobic silicone polymer that forces water to bead and roll off of the car, often without needing wipers. It is sold in 3.5 or 7 oz bottles, or as wipes or towelettes.

Rain-X Online Protectant was introduced to carwashes in June 2005 and is produced by Ecolab. It is a water-based compound that is applied to the entire car's surface, working much like consumer grade Rain-X products.

The original coating has also had use in military and other government settings. The National Oceanic and Atmospheric Administration has used Rain-X in various water repellent research. The Australian Military has examined the effect of Rain-X and similar products to submarine antennae to improve signal transmission, although other coatings had longer-lifespans when submerged in salt-water.

It is also occasionally used in laboratory settings to silanise a surface.

# Chemistry

See also: Superhydrophobe and Lotus effect

Rain-X's primary active ingredient are polysiloxanates, the primary one being hydroxy-terminated polydimethylsiloxane. The polysiloxanes have functional groups that bind to the hydroxyl group of the glass surface.

# Awards

- 2006 Best Brand Award
- Most Innovative New Product, Car Care World Expo 2006
- 2008 Brand Leadership Award, Frost & Sullivan

# External links

- Official website [1]

# Engine stand

## Engine stand

An **engine stand** is a tool commonly used to repair large heavy gasoline or diesel engines. It uses a heavy cantilevered support structure to hold the engine in midair so that the mechanic has access to any exposed surface of the engine.

While small single-piston engines can commonly be laid on a table for repair, a large engine is normally meant to be supported from its engine mounts or from the flywheel transmission case mounts, and fragile components such as oil pans and valve covers would be crushed if the large engine were placed on a flat surface.

Engine stands are typically mounted on large casters so than an engine can be moved around the shop to different test and repair stations, and the engine can often be rotated in midair to provide easier access to underside surfaces of the engine.

The engine stand is commonly used in combination with the engine crane to remove or install an engine in a vehicle, break in that engine, and perform repairs.

### External links

*   Historical example of an early engine stand that could be rotated to permit work on the underside of the engine - *Do It With Tools and Machines*, Popular Science monthly, December 1918, page 67, Scanned by Google Books: http://books.google.com/books?id=EikDAAAAMBAJ&pg=PA67

# 3,000 mile myth

## 3,000 mile myth

The **3,000 mile myth** refers to a common belief that all cars should have their oil changed at least every 3,000 miles to maintain their car engine correctly. Efforts are under way to convince the public that this is not necessary, and that people should follow the advice given in their owner's manual rather than the advice of the oil-change businesses.

Oil being drained from a car.

### History

### Reasons

This recently identified "myth" has continued to exist due to the complexity existing in today's car industry. The diverse array of cars and oil types available make it hard for an average person to reliably know what to do.

In response to this, car manufacturers include a manual with recommendations for how often the oil should be changed often including recommendations based on driving conditions. Some models now come with a monitoring system that alerts the driver when the oil needs changing. Depending on driving conditions, these can extend change intervals to 10,000 or 15,000 miles. In case of diesel engines and manufacturer recommended long-life oil, the indicated change interval can be as long as 19,000 miles (BMW) or 30,000 miles (VW).

### External links

- 3,000 Mile Myth [1]
- General Motors Joins Campaign to Demystify Oil Changes [2]
- How Stuff Works Video Describing the Myth [3]

# Auto electrician

## Auto electrician

An **auto electrician** is a tradesman specializing in electrical wiring of motor vehicles. Auto electricians may be employed in the installation of new electrical components or the maintenance and repair of existing electrical components. Auto electricians specialize in cars and commercial vehicles.

# Interference engine

## Interference engine

An **interference engine** is a type of 4-stroke internal combustion piston engine. Depending on the design of an engine, piston and valve paths may "interfere" with one another as a result of incorrect timing in their movements. (Such designs are also called "interference head" or "non-freewheeling", and include virtually all diesel engines. Conversely, non-interfering engines, such as the Mazda B engine, are called "free-wheeling" or "non-interference" engines.)

In piston engines using poppet valves, the valves descend into the combustion area at the top of the cylinder, while the pistons rise into this area from below. If the lowest point of a valve's descent is lower than the highest point that the piston reaches, the engine is considered an interference engine. In normal operation, the relative timing of the valve and piston's motion prevents them from colliding, but if the valve timing is altered through wear or improper adjustment, or if a valve spring breaks, one or more valves may be placed in the path of a piston.

In interference engine designs, regular belt or chain service is especially important as incorrect timing may result in the pistons and valves colliding and causing extensive engine damage and therefore costly repairs. The piston will likely bend the valves or if a piece of valve or piston is broken off within the cylinder, the broken piece may cause severe damage within the cylinder, possibly affecting the connecting rods. Many manufacturers who were using belts for valve timing have gone back to using chains on new engine offerings, especially on interference designs. However, some non-interference designs have retained belts due to the risk of engine damage from a failure being non-existent. Some manufacturers liked the belt's quietness compared to the chain, and the ability to make additional profits from routine belt service. However, chains, in many cases, last the life of the engine, rarely requiring maintenance and helping to lower the cost of ownership for car buyers who are conscious of that statistic. Also, it was discovered that the sound difference between the two was negligible. During the peak popularity of the belt, chains or cogwheels were used almost exclusively on overhead valve (OHV) engines (which rarely are equipped with belts, regardless of the manufacturer and time of design) and almost all overhead camshaft (OHC) engines received belts. However, chains are lately becoming more popular for OHC designs.

# Sudden unintended acceleration

## Sudden unintended acceleration

**Sudden Unintended Acceleration (SUA)** is the unintended, unexpected, uncontrolled acceleration of a vehicle from a stationary position, low initial speed or at cruising speed, often accompanied by an apparent loss of braking effectiveness. It is often unclear whether problems are caused by driver error, mechanical or electrical problems with automobiles, or some combination of these factors.

### Definition and background

In the 1980s, the National Highway Traffic Safety Administration (NHTSA) reported a narrow definition of sudden acceleration only from near standstill in their 1989 *Sudden Acceleration Report*:

> "Sudden acceleration incidents" (SAI) are defined for the purpose of this report as unintended, unexpected, high-power accelerations from a stationary position or a very low initial speed accompanied by an apparent loss of braking effectiveness. In a typical scenario, the incident begins at the moment of shifting to "Drive" or "Reverse" from "Park".

The report is taken from a study, begun in 1986, in which the NHTSA examined ten vehicles suffering from an "above average" number of incident reports and concluded that those incidents must have resulted from driver error. In the lab tests, throttles were positioned to wide open prior to brake application in an attempt to replicate the circumstances of the incidents under study. However, it is important to note that the newest vehicle involved in the study was a 1986 model and that no test vehicles were equipped with manual transmissions or the electronic control (drive by wire) systems common in 2010.

These tests were meant to simulate reports of the time suggesting that the vehicles were at a standstill and accelerated uncontrollably when shifted from park. With modern drive by wire fuel controls, problems are believed to occur exclusively while the vehicle is under way.

In the 1950s, General Motors automobiles with automatic transmissions placed the R for reverse at the furthest clockwise position in the rotation of the column-mounted shift lever. L for low position was just adjacent as one would move the lever one notch counterclockwise. Because it was very easy to select L, a forward position when desiring R, to reverse, there were many unintended lurches forward while the driver was watching toward the rear, expecting to reverse the automobile. By the 1960s, gear selection arrangements became standardized in the familiar PRNDL, with reverse well away from the forward positions and between the Park and Neutral selections. The elimination of the 'Push-button' drive control on all Chrysler products began after 1965 to eliminate the ease of selecting an unintended direction.

## Possible factors

Sudden unintended acceleration incidents often involve the **simultaneous failure** of a vehicle's acceleration and brake systems. Acceleration system factors may include:

- Pedal misapplication
- Unresponsive (entrapped) pedals
- Electronic throttle control or cruise control failure (see drive by wire)
- Stuck throttle (unrelated to pedal position)

Unintended acceleration resulting from pedal misapplication is a driver error wherein the driver presses the accelerator when braking is intended. Some shorter drivers' feet may not be long enough to touch the floor and pedals, making them more likely to press the wrong pedal due to a lack of proper tactile reference. Pedal misapplication may be related to pedal design and placement, as in cases where the brake and accelerator are too close to one another, or the accelerator pedal too large.

An unresponsive accelerator pedal may result from incursion: i.e. blockage by a foreign object, or any other mechanical interference with the pedal's operation — and may involve the accelerator or brake pedal. Throttle butterfly valves may become sluggish in operation or may stick in the closed position. When the driver pushes harder on the right foot, the valve may "pop" open to a point greater than that wanted by the driver, thus creating too much power and a lurch forward. Special solvent sprays are offered by all manufacturers and aftermarket jobbers to solve this very common problem.

Other problems may be implicated in the case of older vehicles equipped with carburetors. Weak, disconnected, or mis-connected throttle return springs, worn shot-pump barrels, chafed cable housings, and cables which jump their tracks in the throttle-body crank can all cause similar acceleration problems.

For drive-by-wire automobiles, a brake-accelerator interlock switch, or "smart throttle" would eliminate or at least curtail any instance of unintended acceleration not a result of pedal misapplication by causing the brake to override the throttle. An unintended acceleration event would require the failure of such a mechanism if it were present. Such a solution would not be applicable to older vehicles lacking a drive-by-wire throttle.

Analyses conducted in the mid to late 1990s on Jeep Cherokee and Grand Cherokee vehicles concluded that hundreds of reported sudden accelerations in these vehicles were likely caused by an undesired current leakage pathway that resulted in actuation of the cruise control servo. When this occurred, typically at shift engage (moving the shift lever from park to reverse), the engine throttle would move to the wide open position. While the brakes were operational, operator response was often not quick enough to prevent an accident. Most of these events occurred in close confines in which rapid operator response would be necessary to prevent striking a person, fixed object or another vehicle. Many of these events occurred at car washes, and the Jeep Grand Cherokee continues to experience sudden acceleration at car washes across the country. A statistical analysis of SAIs in 1991 through 1995 Jeeps revealed that the root cause of these incidents could not be human error, as had been historically posited by NHTSA and auto manufacturers.

## Effects on braking

The hydraulic brakes found on most family cars and light trucks are designed with a boost system powered by the vacuum generated by the car's engine. This same force is what pulls in air and fuel to power the engine and available braking force is inversely linked to throttle.

Put simply, braking power decreases as throttle increases, and power brakes cannot provide full braking force at high throttle settings. This is true regardless of the cause of the acceleration. More accurately, higher throttle settings reduce the engine's ability to *regenerate* braking power, as brakes retain a reserve of power until used. This reserve is discharged when the brake pedal is pressed and released, after which the brake pedal will become stiffer and braking less effective.

This effect can be safely observed in a parked car, with the engine turned off. For this reason, experts advise drivers against pressing the brake repeatedly in an unintended acceleration event. Rather, drivers should press the brake firmly and hold.

In addition, severe brake fade may be experienced as drivers are forced to apply brakes forcefully and constantly in order to control the vehicle, resulting in excessive heat buildup in the braking system and causing the brakes to lose their effectiveness even when fully applied.

## Reported incidents

Reported incidents of sudden acceleration, include:

- 1988: 1986 Honda Accords were documented to have had sudden acceleration incidents due to the Vehicle Speed Control component, as reported to the NHTSA.
- 1997: Sudden acceleration in Jeep Cherokees and Jeep Grand Cherokees was reported by Diane Sawyer in a March 1997 ABC News Primetime segment.
- 2000: Several Ford Explorers were reported about in the UK by a Channel 4 news program where the vehicle was already moving at speed and experienced sudden acceleration.
- 2006: The 2004 Ford Mustang Cobra [1] was recalled by Ford for accelerator pedals that failed to return to idle after being fully pressed.
- 2008: Incidents involving the 2005 Kia Amanti and Kia Sephia had been reported that were preceded by a racing or highly-revving engine.
- 2009: Toyota Avalon displays unintended acceleration without floor mat; observed by dealer [2]

- 2009-2010: Several vehicles were recalled in the 2009–2010 Toyota vehicle recalls, which resulted in suspension of production and sales of many of Toyota's most popular models, including the Toyota Corolla, Toyota Camry, Toyota Tacoma pickups, Toyota Avalon, Toyota Matrix, Pontiac Vibe, and more.

## Audi 5000

During model years 1982-1987, Audi issued a series of recalls of Audi 5000 models associated with reported incidents of *sudden unintended acceleration* linked to six deaths and 700 accidents. At the time, National Highway Traffic Safety Administration ( NHTSA) was investigating 50 car models from 20 manufacturers for sudden surges of power.

*60 Minutes* aired a report titled *Out of Control* on November 23, 1986, featuring interviews with six people who had sued Audi after reporting unintended acceleration, including footage of an Audi 5000 ostensibly displaying a surge of acceleration while the brake pedal was depressed. Subsequent investigation revealed that *60 Minutes* had not disclosed they had engineered the vehicle's behavior — fitting a canister of compressed air on the passenger-side floor, linked via a hose to a hole drilled into the transmission — the arrangement executed by one of the experts who had testified on behalf of a plaintiff in a then pending lawsuit against Audi's parent company.

Audi contended, prior to findings by outside investigators, that the problems were caused by driver error, specifically pedal misapplication. Subsequently, the National Highway Traffic Safety Administration (NHTSA) concluded that the majority of unintended acceleration cases, including all the ones that prompted the *60 Minutes* report, were caused by driver error such as confusion of pedals. CBS did not acknowledge the test results of involved government agencies, but did acknowledge the similar results of another study.

With the series of recall campaigns, Audi made several modifications; the first adjusted the distance between the brake and accelerator pedal on automatic-transmission models. Later repairs, of 250,000 cars dating back to 1978, added a device requiring the driver to press the brake pedal before shifting out of park. As a byproduct of sudden unintended acceleration, vehicles now include gear stick patterns and brake interlock mechanisms to prevent inadvertent gear selection.

Audi's U.S. sales, which had reached 74,061 in 1985, dropped to 12,283 in 1991 and remained level for three years. — with resale values falling dramatically. Audi subsequently offered increased warranty protection and renamed the affected models — with the *5000* becoming the *100* and *200* in 1989. The company only reached the same level of U.S. sales again by model year 2000.

As of early 2010, a class-action lawsuit filed in 1987 by about 7,500 Audi Audi 5000-model owners remains unsettled and is currently contested in county court in Chicago after appeals at the Illinois state and U.S. federal levels. The plaintiffs in this lawsuit charge that on account of the sudden acceleration controversy, Audis had lost resale value.

The lawsuits surrounding the reported sudden acceleration episodes were a subject of Peter W. Huber's 1993 book, *Galileo's Revenge: Junk Science In The Courtroom.*

## See also

- Automobile safety defect
- Automotive accident
- Electronic stability control, comprehensive drive by wire safety systems
- George Russell Weller
- Product recalls

## External links

- The Mayerson Law Offices, P.C.: Toyota and Lexus Sudden Acceleration Problem [3]
- Toyota unintended acceleration tests, compares Camry with Infiniti [4]
- How To Deal With Unintended Acceleration [5]
- A Short, Sad History of So-Called Sudden Acceleration [6]
- Sudden deceleration [7]

# Engine break-in

## Engine break-in

**Engine break-in**, also known as running in [1], is the procedure of conditioning the new engine of a vehicle by following specific driving guidelines during the first few hours of its use. The focus of breaking-in an engine is on the contact between the piston rings of the engine and the cylinder wall. There is no universal preparation or set of instructions for breaking in an engine. Most importantly, experts disagree on whether it is better to start engines on high or low power to break them in. While there are still consequences to an unsuccessful break-in, they are harder to quantify on modern engines than on older models. People no longer break in the engines of their own vehicles after purchasing a car or motorcycle as the process is done in production.

### Goal

The goal of modern engine break-ins is the settling of piston rings into an engine's cylinder wall. A cylinder wall is not perfectly smooth but has a deliberate slight roughness to help oil adhesion. As the engine is powered up, the piston rings between the pistons and cylinder wall will begin to seal against the wall's small ridges. If the engine is powered up too quickly or not enough (depending on engine), the rings may grind against the ridges and wear them down. The tighter the piston rings are set in, the longer an engine is expected to last.

### Preparation

There are important preparations which must be made before the actual process of running the engine. The break-in can take place either in the vehicle or on an engine stand, which is meant to simulate a vehicle. Each engine has specific preparation needs of its own due to factors such as the many different types of engine models, the vehicles it belongs to, and conflicting expert instructions. For example, each engine should be lubricated and run on oil specified by its designers which can be found in a manual.

# Process

The main area of controversy among engine break-in instructions is whether to run the engine slowly or quickly to initiate the process. Those who promote raising the power settings steadily will recommend changing the engine setting from low to high powers as to not work the engine too hard and create excessive glazing on the cylinder wall (which would require the pistons to be removed and wall fixed). Other experts disagree and believe that to start the engine at a high power is the best way to effectively set in the pistons. The following are examples of how the two processes can be carried out:

## Start high power

Start with Revolutions_per_minute (rpm) between 2500 and 4000, and run the engine for about 15 minutes while watching so that the oil pressure does not get too high, which is dangerous. After changing oil and checking that the engine functions, drive using lower power settings.

A high power setting is relative to the vehicle type, so half as many rpm may be necessary if a car has a smaller cylinder wall.

## Start low power

Setting will be around 1500 rpm, run for about half an hour while like the other method checking oil pressure and begin again should there be any over-boiling of the engine's coolant, which is a combination of air, oil, and water. Once this initial step is completed, drive in varying speeds on the road (or stand) by accelerating between speeds of 30 and 50 miles per hour.

# Consequences

The following are consequences of a bad engine break-in:

1. Oil will be allowed to gather in the cylinder wall, and a vehicle will use much more of it than necessary.

2. If a ring does not set into the grooves of the cylinder wall but creates friction against them each time an engine runs, the cylinder wall will be worn out.

3. Unsuccessfully setting piston rings into a cylinder wall will result in the necessity of new engine parts, or the entire engine depending on how extensive the damage is

# Modern vs. Old Engines

The time it takes to complete an engine break-in procedure has decreased significantly from a number of days to a few hours since modern engines have become more efficient. The factories in which they are produced are also capable of better assembly. For example, older engines had larger ridges in their cylinder walls which made it harder and longer to secure the piston rings within them.

# Reproduction Auto parts

## Reproduction Auto parts

A **reproduction part** is one that has been re-made to original specifications, answering a shortage or replacing an obsolete item that is no longer produced and/or supplied by the manufacturer. It can be a perfect copy of the original or a very close imitation. Such spare parts are commonly referred to as 'repros'.

### Advantages and disadvantages

- The first, obvious advantage is having the item available again, which aides in the restoration of a vehicle to the correct, factory specifications. It also cancels the need to find a good used part otherwise not available new, or the sourcing out of NOS parts (New Old Stock) which can be a difficult, time consuming task and often an expensive one due to their rarity. Many auto manufacturers actually discard or even destroy new parts that have been stocked unused for long periods.
- A common disadvantage of the reproduction part is often the need for it to be produced in industrial quantities requiring mass production using costly tooling, thus prohibiting the reproduction of certain items which may prove uneconomical. As time passes, many vehicles become scarce and large quantity productions are not possible.
- Quality issues may arise when reproducing items. Some suppliers will inevitably reduce the quality of the part to allow for a lower retail price - Keeping in mind auto manufacturers normally produce their items in mass, it is often impossible for a supplier to repeat the process without lowering quantity or quality for obvious reasons.
- Price - Reproductions are sometimes considerably more expensive than the originals, for the reasons listed above.

### Production methods

- There are many methods for reproducing parts, depending on the part, its use and the materials it is made of. One possibility is contacting the OEM who originally made the part and might still have the necessary tooling. In such case, an original part is obtained without the need for a wide research or extensive reverse-engineering.
- Lamp lenses (like headlight lenses, taillight lenses and side marker lenses) can often be produced taking an original item as a master, making molds using liquid resins. There are several drawbacks

to this method, mostly an inferior quality final result, and the difficulty to make lenses incorporating several colors.

- Other parts are made using CNC machining, plastic injection molding, metal stamping etc.

- An extremely accurate repro brings a vehicle close to its original, factory new condition. This is a very important factor in classic auto-shows and concours competitions.

### Distinguishing repros

- A knowledgeable person with a discerning vision can usually distinguish an original part from a non-original part. Different production methods leave different marks on parts. Mold parting lines, machining marks, etc. Some makers go to great lengths and even reproduce the original markings and part numbers originally found on the item. A carefully executed part will be very difficult to distinguish from an original.

## Market overview

- The market of reproduced parts mostly depends, like many other things, on supply and demand. Vehicles that are still quite popular (for example a Ford Mustang or a VW Beetle) have a vast array of parts readily available. Some of them are OEM re-productions and some are newly made, mass produced items. Owners of a rare marque or model will find it more difficult sourcing out new parts. In many cases, vintage or pre-war vehicles have their parts remade as one-offs by professionals. There are some very large retailers of reproduction parts, especially in the U.S.

- Nowadays, the market for repros is a steadily growing field which helps owners and collectors of vintage or rare cars maintain their vehicles in original condition.

# Kal Tire

## Kal Tire

| Type | Private |
|---|---|
| **Founded** | 1953, Vernon, BC, Canada |
| **Headquarters** | Vernon, BC, Canada |
| **Key people** | Thomas J. Foord OBC, Founder |
| | Robert Foord, President |
| **Industry** | Retail Distribution |
| **Products** | Tires and Automotive parts, sales and service |
| **Locations** | 230 [1] (As of July, 2010) |
| **Employees** | 4,000 (As of July, 2010) |
| **Website** | www.kaltire.com [2] |

**Kal Tire** is a wholly owned Canadian company based in Vernon, British Columbia, where it was originally founded in 1953 by Thomas J. Foord OBC. Its business comprises retail tire sales for passenger and light truck vehicles, mechanical services for passenger and light trucks, commercial truck tires, mining and off-road sales and service and retreading of both commercial and off-road tires.

## History

Kal Tire was started in 1953 by Thomas J. FoordOBC with the initial goal of servicing the commercial logging operations that operated in the Okanagan Valley around Vernon, BC and Nakusp, BC with his partner Jim Lockhead by building customers' trust.

Kal Tire was named after Kalamalka Lake, the prominent "Lake of Many Colours" landmark in Vernon. The company is still based in its birthplace of Vernon.

Since 1953, Kal Tire has expanded steadily. Kal Tire comprises 165 company-owned branches, 49 independent associate dealers, 11 mining/industrial/commercial locations, 10 retread facilities, one OTR plant and four distribution warehouses. The business covers a market that includes British Columbia, Alberta, Yukon, Northwest Territories, Saskatchewan, Manitoba, Northern Ontario, parts of Southern Ontario and Quebec, as well as mining operations in Mexico, Argentina, Chile, South

America, The United Kingdom, Ghana and Australia.

# Marketing

Kal Tire started with the motto of 'If we sell it, we guarantee it' which is still used by the company today. That was followed by the slogan of 'You'll like us for more than our tires'. This campaign proved very successful for the company but was then replaced by service stories. Kal Tire currently uses the brand position of 'True Service'.

Participation in industry trade shows and participation in organizations is a key part of the marketing strategy of Kal Tire. Some of the organizations that Kal Tire is associated with include Western Canada Tire Dealers Association, Tire Industry Association and BC Roadbuilders Association.

# Services

## Retail

Kal Tire sells and services many name brand manufacturers including: Bridgestone, Firestone, Michelin, Yokohama, Nokian, Falken, Nitto, Maxxis and Multi-Mile products. Kal Tire also recently expanded its service offering to include mechanical work ranging from shocks and struts to brakes and oil service, but it it not provided at all locations. Mechanical part suppliers include Raybestos friction parts, Truxxx lift and leveling kits, Moog steering parts, Trico wiper blades and Pennzoil. Batteries are also sold for cars, trucks and marine vehicles using the DieHard line of batteries.

## Commercial and industrial

Kal Tire carries a full range of commercial truck tires and is also the largest retreader of commercial tires in Canada with ten retread facilities across Canada that use the Bandag process. Kal Tire also carries and services industrial-use tires for equipment such as forklifts, excavators and tracked vehicles.

## OTR and mining

# External links

- Kal Tire official website [2] - July 9, 2009
- Commitment to Safety - Work Safe BC [3]
- OTR Tyres Official Website [4]
- Western Canada Tire Dealers Association [5]
- Tire Industry Association [6]
- BC Roadbuilders Association [7]

# RTITB National Junior Mechanic Competition 1987

## RTITB National Junior Mechanic Competition 1987

The **1987 National Junior Mechanics Competition (NJMC)** (formerly the Apprentice Competition) event for the Road Transport Industry Training Board (RTITB) National Mechanics Competition was held on 24 June 1987 at MOTEC 1 [1] (Multi Occupational Training and Educational Centre) located at High Ercall, a former RAF base.

The RTITB's Chairman, John Armstrong, revealed that 230 teams entered 1987's National Junior Mechanics Competition (NJMC). After regional heats, quarter-finals and semi-finals the final day consisted of a morning practical round contested by 10 teams, only 4 teams qualified for the final round.

The team from Soundwell Technical College, Bristol, England won the competition for the 4th time, having last beaten the competition in 1981. Carlisle College were place 2nd, after leading in the practical round.

Highlights of the final were shown on Central Television news.

Austin Rover's UK Services Director, Roy Davies, presented the Winner's shield to Soundwell's Team Captain Mark Mannion. The Road Transport Industry Training Board was hit by scandal in 1997 and lost the right to issue TEC (A-level equivalent) certificates. The NJMC competition did not continue after 1997. .

## Practical Round

| RANK | PRACTICAL ROUND | POINTS |
|------|-----------------|--------|
| 1. | Carlisle College | 318 |
| 2. | Soundwell College | 306 |
| 3. | South Devon College | 296 |
| 4. | Stevenson College | 288 |
| 5. | Burton Upon Trent College | 284 |
| 6. | Mid Kent College | 263 |
| 7. | Woolwich College | 256 |
| 8. | Trust Motors (Leeds) | 226 |
| 9. | Chesterfield College | 226 |
| 10. | Suffolk College | 220 |

## Final

| RANK | FINAL | POINTS |
|------|-------|--------|
|  | **Soundwell College**<br>Mark Mannion (Captain)<br>David Gawler<br>Adrian Canham<br>John Smith<br>Ian Headford (Reserve)<br>Mike Newby (Manager) | 42 |
|  | **Carlisle College**<br>Justin Ellis (Captain)<br>Paul Moffat<br>Stephen Hill<br>Andrew Wilson<br>Andrew Hodgson (Reserve)<br>Steve Doughty (Manager)<br>Michael Clarke (Assistant Manager) | 40 |
|  | **South Devon College**<br>Mark Cutmore (Captain)<br>Colin Samsom<br>Andrew Watters<br>Brian Trebilcock<br>Antony Dryland (Reserve)<br>Colin Drew (Manager) | 32 |

| 4. | ⚑ **Stevenson College** | 23 |
|---|---|---|
| | Alan Milne (Captain) | |
| | Douglas Pugh | |
| | Brue Unrau | |
| | Kevin Macaulay | |
| | William Blackley (Reserve) | |
| | Alan Skene(Manager) | |

# Previous Winners

| Year | Winners |
|---|---|
| 1986 | ✛ Beverley College |
| 1985 | ✛ Oxford College |
| 1984 | ✛ Guildford College |

# References

## Bibliography

- *Transport Training, The Newspaper of The Road Transport Industry Training Board*, **107**, Great Britain, 1987

# Article Sources and Contributors

**Car Talk** *Source*: http://en.wikipedia.org/?oldid=390583414 *Contributors*: John

**Jump start (vehicle)** *Source*: http://en.wikipedia.org/?oldid=380868195 *Contributors*: L Kensington

**Timing belt** *Source*: http://en.wikipedia.org/?oldid=389929170 *Contributors*:

**Tire rotation** *Source*: http://en.wikipedia.org/?oldid=380745836 *Contributors*: 1 anonymous edits

**Oil sludge** *Source*: http://en.wikipedia.org/?oldid=374387254 *Contributors*: 1 anonymous edits

**Auto detailing** *Source*: http://en.wikipedia.org/?oldid=387525276 *Contributors*: CZmarlin

**User guide** *Source*: http://en.wikipedia.org/?oldid=383274668 *Contributors*: Mikeo

**Car wash** *Source*: http://en.wikipedia.org/?oldid=386543344 *Contributors*: 1 anonymous edits

**Grease gun (tool)** *Source*: http://en.wikipedia.org/?oldid=386734381 *Contributors*:

**Back-fire** *Source*: http://en.wikipedia.org/?oldid=385120820 *Contributors*: Uruiamme

**Cold inflation pressure** *Source*: http://en.wikipedia.org/?oldid=333062032 *Contributors*: Redfoxseo

**Haynes Manual** *Source*: http://en.wikipedia.org/?oldid=373426205 *Contributors*: RHaworth

**Wheel alignment** *Source*: http://en.wikipedia.org/?oldid=382193855 *Contributors*:

**Auto mechanic** *Source*: http://en.wikipedia.org/?oldid=390636187 *Contributors*:

**Cutting compound** *Source*: http://en.wikipedia.org/?oldid=364770312 *Contributors*: GoingBatty

**Full service** *Source*: http://en.wikipedia.org/?oldid=390319232 *Contributors*: Wintonian

**Automotive restoration** *Source*: http://en.wikipedia.org/?oldid=390273379 *Contributors*: CZmarlin

**Fuel starvation** *Source*: http://en.wikipedia.org/?oldid=366141172 *Contributors*: YSSYguy

**Engine cart** *Source*: http://en.wikipedia.org/?oldid=359254868 *Contributors*: Moorsmur

**VAG-COM** *Source*: http://en.wikipedia.org/?oldid=379735252 *Contributors*:

**Breakdown (vehicle)** *Source*: http://en.wikipedia.org/?oldid=381030889 *Contributors*: Jayjg

**Auto maintenance** *Source*: http://en.wikipedia.org/?oldid=388381991 *Contributors*: 1 anonymous edits

**Plastic headlight restoration** *Source*: http://en.wikipedia.org/?oldid=378039724 *Contributors*: 1 anonymous edits

**Chilton Company** *Source*: http://en.wikipedia.org/?oldid=365780711 *Contributors*: George H. Buzby

**Car ramp** *Source*: http://en.wikipedia.org/?oldid=270900306 *Contributors*:

**Remote diagnostics** *Source*: http://en.wikipedia.org/?oldid=365626529 *Contributors*: Gor1420

**The Garage (TV)** *Source*: http://en.wikipedia.org/?oldid=390372081 *Contributors*: Trjp

**Paintless dent repair** *Source*: http://en.wikipedia.org/?oldid=386015610 *Contributors*: Johnuniq

**Service (motor vehicle)** *Source*: http://en.wikipedia.org/?oldid=388674209 *Contributors*:

**Eastwood Company** *Source*: http://en.wikipedia.org/?oldid=390649429 *Contributors*: Chowbok

**Service Labor Time Standards** *Source*: http://en.wikipedia.org/?oldid=333823950 *Contributors*: Abductive

**Tune-up** *Source*: http://en.wikipedia.org/?oldid=338666996 *Contributors*: 1 anonymous edits

**Number matching** *Source*: http://en.wikipedia.org/?oldid=389834386 *Contributors*:

**Technical Service Bulletin** *Source*: http://en.wikipedia.org/?oldid=386715881 *Contributors*: Philip Trueman

**Italian tuneup** *Source*: http://en.wikipedia.org/?oldid=316870475 *Contributors*:

**Deglazing (engine mechanics)** *Source*: http://en.wikipedia.org/?oldid=355601611 *Contributors*:

**Engine crane** *Source*: http://en.wikipedia.org/?oldid=379207744 *Contributors*: Malcolma

**Turtle Wax** *Source*: http://en.wikipedia.org/?oldid=390569587 *Contributors*:

**Rain-X** *Source*: http://en.wikipedia.org/?oldid=387383281 *Contributors*: Shadowjams

**Engine stand**  *Source*: http://en.wikipedia.org/?oldid=379207813  *Contributors*: Malcolma

**3,000 mile myth**  *Source*: http://en.wikipedia.org/?oldid=383874086  *Contributors*: Shell Kinney

**Auto electrician**  *Source*: http://en.wikipedia.org/?oldid=352917125  *Contributors*: Malcolma

**Interference engine**  *Source*: http://en.wikipedia.org/?oldid=390069154  *Contributors*: Egil

**Sudden unintended acceleration**  *Source*: http://en.wikipedia.org/?oldid=388018568  *Contributors*:

**Engine break-in**  *Source*: http://en.wikipedia.org/?oldid=383799979  *Contributors*: Zee991

**Reproduction Auto parts**  *Source*: http://en.wikipedia.org/?oldid=380399710  *Contributors*: 1 anonymous edits

**Kal Tire**  *Source*: http://en.wikipedia.org/?oldid=386951621  *Contributors*:

**RTITB National Junior Mechanic Competition 1987**  *Source*: http://en.wikipedia.org/?oldid=388302825  *Contributors*: Here2helpU

# Image Sources, Licenses and Contributors

**Image:Car Talk Dewey, Cheetham & Howe.jpg** *Source*: http://en.wikipedia.org/w/index.php?title=File:Car_Talk_Dewey,_Cheetham_&_Howe.jpg *License*: GNU Free Documentation License *Contributors*: Original uploader was Gbleem at en.wikipedia

**Image:CrocodileClamponBattery.jpg** *Source*: http://en.wikipedia.org/w/index.php?title=File:CrocodileClamponBattery.jpg *License*: Public Domain *Contributors*: Original uploader was Wtshymanski at en.wikipedia

**Image:Slave Receptacle.JPG** *Source*: http://en.wikipedia.org/w/index.php?title=File:Slave_Receptacle.JPG *License*: GNU Free Documentation License *Contributors*: CatCube (talk). Original uploader was CatCube at en.wikipedia

**Image:Timing belt.jpg** *Source*: http://en.wikipedia.org/w/index.php?title=File:Timing_belt.jpg *License*: unknown *Contributors*: User:L-Cain

**Image:Timing belt RB30E.jpg** *Source*: http://en.wikipedia.org/w/index.php?title=File:Timing_belt_RB30E.jpg *License*: unknown *Contributors*: -

**Image:Wagga Carwash.jpg** *Source*: http://en.wikipedia.org/w/index.php?title=File:Wagga_Carwash.jpg *License*: unknown *Contributors*: -

**Image:Inside a car wash.jpg** *Source*: http://en.wikipedia.org/w/index.php?title=File:Inside_a_car_wash.jpg *License*: Creative Commons Attribution-Sharealike 2.5 *Contributors*: Hu Totya, Wst, Xnatedawgx

**Image:orscarwash.jpg** *Source*: http://en.wikipedia.org/w/index.php?title=File:Orscarwash.jpg *License*: Creative Commons Attribution 2.5 *Contributors*: Original uploader was Orcaman at en.wikipedia

**Image:Touchless Car Wash.jpg** *Source*: http://en.wikipedia.org/w/index.php?title=File:Touchless_Car_Wash.jpg *License*: GNU Free Documentation License *Contributors*: Original uploader was Sulfur at en.wikipedia

**Image:Bikini Hummer Wash - From Auckland - New Zealand.jpg** *Source*: http://en.wikipedia.org/w/index.php?title=File:Bikini_Hummer_Wash_-_From_Auckland_-_New_Zealand.jpg *License*: Creative Commons Attribution 2.0 *Contributors*: Mark from Auckland, New Zealand

**Image:Grease Gun US Dep. of Labour.jpg** *Source*: http://en.wikipedia.org/w/index.php?title=File:Grease_Gun_US_Dep._of_Labour.jpg *License*: unknown *Contributors*: -

**Image:Flaming Corser.jpg** *Source*: http://en.wikipedia.org/w/index.php?title=File:Flaming_Corser.jpg *License*: Creative Commons Attribution-Sharealike 2.0 *Contributors*: Richard Mushet

**Image:Auto Mechanic.jpg** *Source*: http://en.wikipedia.org/w/index.php?title=File:Auto_Mechanic.jpg *License*: Public Domain *Contributors*: User Interiot on en.wikipedia

**Image:1949 VW Beetle.jpg** *Source*: http://en.wikipedia.org/w/index.php?title=File:1949_VW_Beetle.jpg *License*: Public Domain *Contributors*: Original uploader was Pfan70 at en.wikipedia

**Image:Apperson Chummy Restored By Louie Floyd Apperson.jpg** *Source*: http://en.wikipedia.org/w/index.php?title=File:Apperson_Chummy_Restored_By_Louie_Floyd_Apperson.jpg *License*: Public Domain *Contributors*: Original uploader was ArcticTern at en.wikipedia

**Image:Ford Boss 302 engine.jpg** *Source*: http://en.wikipedia.org/w/index.php?title=File:Ford_Boss_302_engine.jpg *License*: GNU Free Documentation License *Contributors*: User:Morven

**Image:1969 red Shelby Mustang GT350 side.JPG** *Source*: http://en.wikipedia.org/w/index.php?title=File:1969_red_Shelby_Mustang_GT350_side.JPG *License*: Creative Commons Attribution-Sharealike 3.0 *Contributors*: User:BrokenSphere

**Image:Corvette-je-1958.jpg** *Source*: http://en.wikipedia.org/w/index.php?title=File:Corvette-je-1958.jpg *License*: GNU Free Documentation License *Contributors*: Mattes, Rocket000, Saperaud, Sfoskett

**Image:Late model Ford Model T.jpg** *Source*: http://en.wikipedia.org/w/index.php?title=File:Late_model_Ford_Model_T.jpg *License*: GNU Free Documentation License *Contributors*: Rmhermen

**Image:1949 VW dash .jpg** *Source*: http://en.wikipedia.org/w/index.php?title=File:1949_VW_dash_.jpg *License*: Public Domain *Contributors*: Original uploader was Pfan70 at en.wikipedia

**Image:London Feb 10 2008 CoS protest AB 13.JPG** *Source*: http://en.wikipedia.org/w/index.php?title=File:London_Feb_10_2008_CoS_protest_AB_13.JPG *License*: unknown *Contributors*: -

**Image:Oil Change oil pan 2005 gmc suv.JPG** *Source*: http://en.wikipedia.org/w/index.php?title=File:Oil_Change_oil_pan_2005_gmc_suv.JPG *License*: Public Domain *Contributors*: User:Myke2020

**File:Flag of the United Kingdom.svg** *Source*: http://en.wikipedia.org/w/index.php?title=File:Flag_of_the_United_Kingdom.svg *License*: Public Domain *Contributors*: User:Zscout370

**File:CarService.JPG** *Source*: http://en.wikipedia.org/w/index.php?title=File:CarService.JPG *License*: unknown *Contributors*: -

**File:Flag of England.svg** *Source*: http://en.wikipedia.org/w/index.php?title=File:Flag_of_England.svg *License*: Public Domain *Contributors*: User:Nickshanks

**File:Flag of Scotland.svg** *Source*: http://en.wikipedia.org/w/index.php?title=File:Flag_of_Scotland.svg *License*: Public Domain *Contributors*: User:Kbolino

CPSIA information can be obtained at www.ICGtesting.com
Printed in the USA
LVOW03s2151220615

443473LV00006B/42/P